THE TEXAS DIVORCE HANDBOOK

Volume 2: **25 Dirty Tricks to Recognize and Guard Against**

BRYAN JOSEPH FAGAN

THE TEXAS DIVORCE HANDBOOK VOLUME 2:

25 Dirty Tricks to Recognize And Guard Against

BRYAN JOSEPH FAGAN

"The only alternative to coexistence is co-destruction."
—Jawaharlal Nehru, First Prime Minister of India

The Texas Divorce Guide: 25 Dirty Tricks to Recognize and Guard Against is a guide to help you spot tricks sometimes played in divorce and provides some methods to potentially counter them. Use it accordingly—mark it up, fold down the pages, highlight important topics, make notes in the margins, and pass it along to a friend in need. Use it as it was intended to be used—as a guide for those in search of answers.

Do NOT, however, allow this book to take the place of consulting an actual Texas divorce lawyer and sharing the specific facts and circumstances of your situation. Nothing can take the place of a live consultation with a knowledgeable attorney.
Therefore, I'm offering a free consultation with an attorney at my law firm, a $375 value, to encourage you to find the answers you need to navigate toward a successful future.

Call our office today:
(281) 720-3646
www.bryanfagan.com
Call to make your appointment for a
FREE 60-MINUTE consultation today
– A $375 Value –

For additional information contact:
Bryan Fagan
Law Office of Bryan Fagan
3707 Cypress Creek Pkwy suite 400
Houston, TX 77068
Tel: (281) 720-3646
Fax: (855) 668-0536
www.bryanfagan.com

FIRST EDITION
ISBN-13: 978-1-7328903-0-5 (Law Office of Bryan Fagan)
ISBN-10: 1-7328903-0-7

Legal Disclaimer
This Book is Not Legal Advice

TABLE OF CONTENTS

INTRODUCTION

As with my first book, *The Texas Divorce Handbook: Your Step-by-Step Guide to Successfully Navigating Texas Divorce*, this book is an aggregated, curated, and updated version of some of my most popular blog posts from the past few years.

This book was not written to encourage the use of any tricks. Instead, it was written to educate and serve as a warning of things to be on the lookout for.

The theme of this book involves many of the divorce tricks I have witnessed. The stories in this book are composites of what has happened to real people in real courtrooms. The stories are loosely based upon real cases; however, for ethical reasons, the names, facts, and sometimes gender have been changed to protect the identities of all involved.

Any resemblance these stories bear to any past or present client I may have had during my career is purely coincidental.

Having worked as a divorce attorney, I have had the benefit of seeing exactly what litigation does to people over time. I have seen what happens when love turns to hate, and hope turns to fear and distrust.

Divorce and Family Law is an incredibly humbling business. I like to say that I get to meet people at the worst times in their life and help them. When we give job interviews, we ask our potential new hires how they handle stress. We tell them that when they answer the phone, they may, one minute, be talking with someone who thinks they are a hero and a few minutes later, have someone yelling at them because their spouse just turned off the utilities. My consults sometimes ask about our win and loss ratio. However, unlike other areas of the law, divorce and family law is not as clear-cut as that.

A divorce by its very nature generally involves a couple whose resources are no longer pooled, and where costs are now doubled. Where once two incomes covered a mortgage, now there may be a mortgage and an apartment to pay for as well as two electric bills and two grocery bills.

In families with children, a divorced couple now means additional transportation costs as the children are transported back and forth between homes. Parents must also now furnish two different rooms for the children. The cost of living has easily doubled.

What I do believe in, is striving to provide excellent customer service to my clients. I believe that the journey begins by educating my clients. In my first book, I tried to provide a broad overview of the divorce process.

In this book, I will delve a little deeper and explore 25 Dirty Tricks that sometimes come up in a divorce. Unfortunately, getting a divorce is not always straight-forward for every couple. I generally try and put things into perspective for my potential clients by telling them, "Divorce is as easy as the two spouses involved make it. I can get you divorced as fast as the slowest person in the relationship." When couples are upfront, honest and amicable with each other, the divorce can go smoothly. However, most couples are not that fortunate.

My observation is that because some spouses fear getting an unfavorable outcome such as losing custody, paying more support, etc., they behave badly to win their case. People who are fearful can be dangerous.

If not protected, you could face many problems with your divorce case. Unfortunately, some spouses approach divorce with a winner-take-all attitude. These spouses may do this out of anger, fear, guilt, or possibly sadness. Whatever the reason, the results are the same—bank accounts get cleaned out, children are caught in the middle of their warring parents, assets are hidden, or some other sort of bad behavior. Do not allow this to happen to you during your divorce.

When one spouse starts playing these games, there is often a domino effect. A spouse will do one thing such as cutting off the utilities and the other spouse responds by cleaning out the checking account. The next thing you know, you no longer have an uncontested divorce and your divorce proceedings are an all-out war.

This book will illustrate the top 25 dirty divorce tricks we have come across in our office. Hopefully, these stories help prepare you for the tricks some spouses can engage in during a divorce. What you do not know can hurt you, especially if your spouse knows and you do not.

History can be a great teacher. Someone else's experiences can help teach you lessons others learned the hard way. Knowing about these possible tricks is half the battle. Once identified, preventive or corrective action can be taken.

CHAPTER 1

USING THE SAME DIVORCE LAWYER

One of the most frequently asked questions that I hear is, "Can my spouse and I use the same attorney for our uncontested divorce?" The answer is no. Whether your divorce is contested or uncontested, an attorney can only represent one party.

I have decided this trick needs its own chapter because many of the divorce tricks we discuss could easily have been prevented if both parties had been represented by an attorney experienced in family law and divorce.

Many couples believe that they can both hire the same lawyer because they assume that they agree on everything. They expect that the attorney will draft a short document which they can each sign, and they will be divorced.

A Texas divorce is more complicated than that.

What is involved in a Texas Divorce?

In Texas, a divorce, in its purest form, terminates a marriage, giving a married couple the legal right to marry another person.

What many people do not know is that a divorce is a lawsuit that does more than end a marriage. A Texas divorce takes care of three things:

- **Property**—divides marital assets and debts
- **Children**—determines the rights and duties of parents toward children, parental visitation, and establishes child support
- **Marriage**—ends the marriage

Why can't we hire the same lawyer?

The big reason a Texas divorce lawyer can only represent one spouse is that there is a conflict of interest. What is best for one spouse is not necessarily best for the other spouse.

For example, what happens if a disagreement arises which neither spouse contemplated but which must be resolved? If the attorney, who has been hired, knows how to address the disputed issue and by doing so benefits one spouse over the other, this would place the attorney in an ethical dilemma.

To avoid these ethical dilemmas, Texas law does not allow divorce attorneys to represent both spouses in a divorce.

What if only one spouse hires an attorney?

If only one spouse hires an attorney, the retained attorney will only represent one spouse. I have seen this handled a few ways.

Do not think your spouse's attorney also represents you

A spouse who has hired an attorney might try to get the other spouse to use their lawyer for convenience and to save legal fees.

However, the real motive is to gain an unfair advantage during the divorce process by having his or her lawyer "represent both sides."

When couples agree to only hire one lawyer, they must fully understand that the lawyer's duty is to diligently represent only one client's best interests and provide legal advice *only* to the spouse who hired the attorney and signed the representation agreement.

That spouse who hired the attorney gets all the benefits of the knowledge, experience, and guidance of the lawyer. The other gets nothing and is representing him or herself.

Best-Case Scenario

I have seen parties where one spouse hired an attorney and the attorney drafted their agreement. For example, in a case where a husband was represented, and the wife did not have an attorney, the situation was resolved in mediation. The husband's attorney drafted a final divorce decree that they believed accurately reflected what the parties agreed upon. The wife took the agreement and had it reviewed by another attorney. The attorney informed her that although, the divorce decree did reflect the mediated settlement agreement, it was slanted in favor of the husband.

In other words, even if something is drafted that accurately reflects what two spouses agreed upon, there are ways to draft that agreement in favor of one spouse over another. The husband's attorney was looking out for his interest and not his wife's interest.

An example of this could be if the husband was supposed to pay the wife $5,000. This could be placed in the decree that he was supposed to pay her but never put a deadline for that payment.

One reason this might be done is if the husband runs into some financial troubles, he would have some breathing room to meet his obligation without getting in trouble with the court.

Another example is drafting a deed that transfers the wife's interest in some property to the husband but does not draft anything requiring the husband to pay the mortgage or to take the loan out of the wife's name. This would mean that if the husband stops paying the loan, the wife would have no recourse against the husband.

Worst-Case Scenario

It may be that both your spouse and their attorney are against you. This could mean they get:

- More property than you agreed upon
- Additional child support
- You have less visitation than you thought you had
- No decision-making rights regarding the children

Husband Did Not Hire a Lawyer and is Now Stuck With a $600,000 Mistake

Recently an attorney friend and I got into a discussion regarding the differences between contractual alimony and statutory alimony. He had just recently met with a potential client. This potential client did not have an attorney during his divorce. His wife had convinced him to share her attorney so that he could save money.

During the divorce, the wife and her attorney convinced him to pay contractual alimony for $5,000 a month for 120 months after the divorce. The husband at the time had a good paying job and was feeling generous, so he agreed to the request. A year after the divorce, he lost his job and could no longer afford $5,000 a month.

The ex-husband wanted to modify his obligation to his ex-wife to reflect his current income. Unfortunately for this ex-husband, his ex-wife and her attorney were not looking out for his best interest and did not leave him any room to modify his alimony payments. He was stuck for the next ten years paying her $5,000 a month.

It would have been a good idea to hire an attorney before he committed himself to a $600,000 obligation.

Watch out for a Universal Waiver of Service

One way I have seen the problems occur with using the "same attorney "is when that attorney asks the non-client to sign a universal waiver.

5

Every person in Texas is entitled to notice of a divorce lawsuit. This is often accomplished by service of a copy of the lawsuit that was filed with the court. However, personal service is not the only way to bring a divorcing spouse under the power of the court so that the court can make orders regarding a married couple.

Alternatively, a person can waive their right to be personally served with a copy of the lawsuit by signing a Waiver of Service. The waiver of service must be signed in the presence of a notary, notarized, and then filed with the court.

It says you do not want to be served by a process server or constable/sheriff or by certified mail sent by the district clerk.

Should I Sign A Waiver of Service?

I would strongly caution a spouse going through a divorce to **not** sign a Waiver of Service.

One reason is that there are different types of waivers of service and some are known as a universal "Waiver Service," which has clauses included in the waiver of service that will affect your rights concerning the divorce or other court proceedings.

Some of the bad waivers out there mean that once you sign them, you are effectively telling the judge in this case:

- You do not want to be served by a process server or constable/sheriff
- You do not need to be made aware of any court dates

- The judge can sign whatever orders your spouse presents to the judge without further notice to you. In other words, your spouse wins

What Should I File Instead of a Waiver of Service?
Generally, it is a better idea to:

- File an answer and
- Counterpetition in your case.

This is vital if there is something within the marriage that you may want to be confirmed as yours.

There could be separate property, issues concerning children of the marriage, community property, or even community debt that you are telling the court you do not care what happens to.

Signing a bad waiver of service is a serious issue. You can lose property rights, child custody rights, and can even take all the debt.

For those reasons and more, do you still think you should sign a waiver of service?

CHAPTER 2

DO-IT-YOURSELF DIVORCE

Doing your own divorce is a very difficult task. I have heard it compared to trying to perform surgery in the dark. Another comparison I like is that it may be possible to do your own brain surgery, but it is probably not a good idea.

Yes, it may be possible to do your own divorce. However, as some of the following stories will illustrate, seemingly small things can amount to huge mistakes. I have heard other lawyers say that if the following criteria are met, a divorce kit might work:

- No children
- No property
- Short-term marriage (less than three years)
- Young couple
- No assets
- No special assets (pensions, 401ks, businesses, etc.)

Even if these above criteria are met, I would be concerned with trying to handle a divorce on your own. When talking with

9

potential consults, I often find some wrinkle in their case that they overlook.

For example, one consult I met with told me they did not have any children. This turned out not to be the case. The consult had children with other men, but they were not her husband's, so she thought they didn't count.

This type of thinking often extends to property. A consult will think:

- It is my property
- It is in my name
- I made the money that purchased the property

Beware the $200 and $500 Divorce

After signing up, two different clients in less than a month who had had problems with divorce lawyers who had promised to handle their cases at exceptionally low fees and then did not come through, I decided to include a section on minimum court fees.

Beware $200-dollar Divorces

My practice does not offer a divorce for $200, and I do not know any legitimate attorney or website that does. There is a simple reason for this; the filing for a divorce currently costs:

1. $268.00 with no children—Harris County
2. $295 with children—Harris County
3. $292.00 Family Law Case—Montgomery County

This filing fee does not include any additional fees such as the cost of a citation or hiring a process server. This disparity between the cost to file for divorce and what is being advertised illustrates there is no way to get a divorce for as low as $200.

Be Careful of $500 Divorces

My practice does not offer a divorce for $500. I have seen some websites offering a $500 package.

Forms are mailed to you and then you are expected to figure our what to do with them yourself. If you are lucky, the forms may come with instruction. I will caution you that if you are planning to use any forms not prepared by an attorney, use the forms put out by the Texas Supreme Court.

At least once a week, I see someone trying to do their divorce themselves. One of the biggest mistakes that are made by these individuals is that they try and use forms that are not Texas Specific. In one of the cases I absorbed last week, the judge did not let the couple go forward because their divorce decree talked about custody and had some weird non-Texas possession schedule. The Judge told the couple he was not going to let them go forward because 1) we have conservatorship in Texas, not custody; and 2) The possession schedule was not something he would approve. The Judge then told the couple they needed an attorney.

I am not going to discuss the forms put out by the Texas Supreme Court other than to say **pay attention to the boxes.** The forms do not cover a lot of situations. Even if your case seems simple, they were not designed to cover certain circumstances. In the situations in "not included," there are boxes on the forms **WARNING** not to use the forms and to consult with an attorney.

I get at least one case a month, where an individual did not read the **WARNING** box or ignored the box. Then he went before the judge, and because of his set of facts, the judge refused to let him proceed and told him to consult with a divorce attorney.

Story #1—$300 Divorce Cost a Man $100,000

Earlier this week, I received a call from an ex-husband who had divorced his wife in June of 2015. He and his wife agreed that he could have a life insurance policy on her. They continued to live together after the divorce, until the ex-wife died in December 2015. Just that week, he had received a letter from the insurance company informing him that his claim on the $100,000 policy was being denied because of the divorce.

Further questions revealed that the man did not want to pay for an attorney and instead spent $300 for some forms and had done the divorce himself. The ex-husband wanted to know if there was anything that could be done as he had been paying on the policy for over ten years. Unfortunately, in his case, the law does not favor him as I will discuss below.

Failure to Change the Beneficiary of a Life Insurance Policy

It is essential to change the beneficiary on your life insurance policy after a divorce in Texas.

It is not uncommon for people to forget to change their beneficiary designations after a divorce. For this reason, the Texas legislature passed a law to address the situation. Texas Family Code §9.301 specifically sets out provisions to deal with a case where a pre-divorce designation of an ex-spouse as a beneficiary of life insurance benefits has been made.

Under this statute, a pre-divorce designation of a former spouse is not effective UNLESS:

- the decree designates the insured's former spouse as the beneficiary;
- the insured re-designates the former spouse as the beneficiary after the rendition of the divorce decree; or
- the former spouse is designated to receive the proceeds in trust for, on behalf of, or for the benefit of a child or a dependent of either former spouse.

An ex-spouse will not be able to collect on the pre-divorce life insurance policy unless they meet one of the three preceding criteria.

Instead, according to Texas Family Code §9.301 Section (b), the proceeds of the policy are payable to the named alternative beneficiary or, if there is not a named alternative beneficiary, to the estate of the insured.

Keep in mind that if the insurance company is not informed that the parties have divorced, and the ex-spouse should not be paid the benefits, it is possible the insurance company may pay the former spouse. In such a case, it could be costly and difficult to recover the money.

What can be done if an ex-spouse is still designated as beneficiary?

The best thing to do after your divorce would be to contact your life insurance company and to update the beneficiary designations on retirement plans, life insurance policies, annuities, survivor's benefits, and all similar benefit plans.

Alternatively, if the insured has passed away, then one thing that can be done to stop an insurance company from paying a former spouse after the death of an insured is to give written notice by certified mail to the insurer at its home office that the designation of the former spouse is not valid under the Texas Family Code §9.301.

What could the ex-husband have done to prevent his predicament?

In the husband's case, he could either have made sure a provision was placed in the divorce decree designating him as a beneficiary of the insurance policy. Alternatively, after the divorce, he could have contacted the insurance company and had forms signed that had him re-designated as a beneficiary.

The "Cheap and Easy" Online Divorce Is Usually Anything But...

The internet is a great source for referencing information, learning a new recipe, and updating your friends on the latest and greatest coffee shop in town. However, it's been my experience that looking for answers to your divorce problems online is not only a potential mistake, but a costly one as well.

A situation that is familiar enough to divorce attorneys, begins with the parties to a divorce striking a deal between themselves to file for an "uncontested" divorce. They agree to their terms and just want to make things official with the court, but what often ends up happening, is that the parties fail to consider a potential issue regarding the custody of their child(ren), or a debt that is not transferred correctly to the other spouse. Seeking advice from an attorney on these and similar subjects in advance, has the potential to impact you and your spouse in a positive fashion.

Often, these quick and easy divorce websites will provide you with nothing but the same forms that you can receive for free from your local district clerk. These websites will also not be providing you with the advice and counsel that a licensed and experienced attorney can provide you the steps in completing the initial court filings.

Another near-universal truth, regarding these websites that offer quick and easy divorces with "customer support and service" is that there is no guarantee that the person on the other end of the phone or chat screen is a divorce attorney. Quite the contrary, it is likely that the person is not a lawyer at all, and it is even less likely that the person is a lawyer licensed in Texas. The fine print of these cheap and easy online divorces can ultimately cost you hundreds to thousands of dollars in the long run.

CHAPTER 3

DO I NEED A LAWYER TO GET A DIVORCE?

Many people believe that a divorce in Texas should be easy, and that it is just a status change ending the marriage and it does not directly impact other issues. However, this is not the case. A divorce in Texas requires that property, debts, and children, also be considered along with the status change from married to divorce. You cannot get divorced without dealing with these other issues.

Many people file for divorce in Texas without the assistance of an attorney. The internet is an amazing thing. If you search long enough, you can find all the necessary documents online that are required to receive a divorce in Texas. There is no law stating that you absolutely must have an attorney's assistance in filing and a court will grant your divorce without a lawyer representing you. It can be done.

Do I legally have to hire a lawyer to obtain a divorce in Texas?

No, there is no legal requirement that you hire a lawyer for your divorce in Texas.

Five reasons that a person should consider hiring a divorce lawyer include:

- Expert advice
- Reduce stress
- Avoid mistakes
- Binding agreement
- Avoid delays

Can I use the same attorney for both my custody case and my divorce?

Yes. A divorce decree takes care of more than just the termination of the marriage. It is mandatory that if there are children, that the children be included in the divorce.

In other words, orders will be established to cover children's issues such as:

- Where will the children live?
- What will visitation look like?
- Medical support
- Child support
- Decision making

Can I do the divorce myself in Texas?

The answer depends on several factors, including the personalities of you and your spouse and the importance of what is at stake.

Though it is not recommended, some people choose not to use divorce lawyers to handle their divorce. If you have any issues relating to property distribution, children, or claims to alimony, do not complete a divorce without consulting an attorney.

Why should I hire a divorce lawyer?
Whether a party really needs a divorce lawyer depends on the facts of the case. Lawyers are professionals and know their area of law very well. They can offer you their advice and expertise throughout your divorce.

Divorce lawyers will also see problems, pitfalls, and issues that may not occur to divorcing spouses who are representing themselves. Examples include:

- Custody arrangements
- Division of property issues
- Child support enforcement issues
- Alimony issues
- Tax treatment
- Exercising possession of and access to your children
- Discovery of hidden assets

An analogy that I like to use is: "Although you can perform your own surgery, it is generally a better idea if you go to a doctor instead."

How important is having an attorney
for your divorce in Texas?

As stated earlier, many people file for divorce in Texas without the assistance of an attorney. The necessary documents that you'll need to get a divorce in Texas are online. There is, also, no law stating you absolutely must have an attorney's assistance in filing the papers, and a court will grant your divorce without a lawyer representing you. It can be done.

It is my opinion, however, that you should have an attorney when the time comes to file for divorce. I know, it's shocking to hear that an attorney would advise you to hire an attorney for your divorce. Stay with me, though. There are advantages to having a divorce attorney by your side that goes beyond simply having someone else do the lion's share of the work for you.

If my spouse has a divorce lawyer, do I need one?

No, but you probably should have your own lawyer if your spouse has already retained his (or her) own divorce attorney. Although divorces in Texas happen all the time with one or even no lawyers involved, that does not mean it is necessarily in your best interest to go without one.

It is a good idea for each party in a divorce to hire a divorce lawyer. Generally, when one person is represented, and the other spouse is not, the spouse that is represented does better in the divorce. The most one-sided agreements I have seen, have been when one spouse has a divorce lawyer, and the other does not. If both spouses are represented there is a better opportunity for both sides to come to a reasonable agreement.

Can we hire one lawyer to do the divorce?

A divorce lawyer can only represent one spouse in a divorce. When one spouse separately hires a divorce lawyer, the lawyer only has a duty to the spouse that hired him. The divorce lawyer has no duty to the other spouse and may even have a duty to act to the detriment of the other spouse when it is permissible and to the benefit of the spouse who hired the lawyer.

However, if you agree on all issues, the attorney can prepare papers for their client based on that agreement. The other party does not have to get a separate attorney.

What should I look for in a divorce attorney?

Having an attorney to represent you in your divorce is one of the most important aspects of a successful case. Your personal knowledge of divorce is based on stories you have probably heard from friends or family members, and as a result, you don't know what to expect.

That's fine. You've never been divorced before and, as I tell clients all the time, hopefully, you never have to talk to another family law attorney again. The fact remains that if you do have to go through a divorce, you should be represented by an effective and experienced family law attorney.

The following are some characteristics I believe a family law attorney should embody:

- The ability to communicate
- Willingness to negotiate
- Honesty

- Experience in advocacy
- Credentials
- Location

The ability to communicate

The key to any good relationship is the ability to communicate. Whether your attorney is communicating a legal argument to a judge or is simply updating you on the drafting of a document, the transfer of knowledge from your attorney's brain to your ears is critical.

Willingness to Negotiate

Television and movies would have us believe that most lawsuits wind up before a judge where the lawyers duke it out verbally with one another for all the world to see. If we can tap the breaks on this image for a moment, I'm here to tell you that most lawsuits (including divorces) settle long before a court date is even necessary.

Honesty

Lawyers have a bad reputation for not always being honest, but from my experience, I can safely say that the vast majority of attorneys that I have encountered are fair and do seek to put their client's interests ahead of their own. If you are in the market for a family law attorney, it is critical to have a conversation with the attorney before hiring him or her.

Experience in Advocacy

Family law attorneys spend more time in court than almost any other kind of attorney. However, this does not mean that the family law attorney you are set to hire actually has extensive courtroom experience. While a hearing or trial can certainly be won or lost during the preparation stage, a lawyer should also be a strong advocate in the courtroom for their client.

Credentials

The most important thing to look for in selecting a divorce or family lawyer in Texas is that they are licensed to practice in the state where the case is ongoing.

Clients sometimes come to me who have a case in a state other than Texas. Unfortunately, depending on the circumstances, I may not be able to help them and will need to refer them to an attorney licensed to practice in that state. There are times, however, when I can help them because the facts of their case are such that we can open a case in Texas and move forward.

Location

Another thing to consider when hiring a divorce or family lawyer is where they are located. My office is positioned in North Houston in the Spring, Texas area. My office is about halfway between Conroe, Texas and Houston, Texas. As a result, about half my family law and divorce cases are either in Montgomery County or Harris County.

I do practice in other counties in Texas and have taken cases in locations such as Waco, TX and Dallas, TX. However, before taking those cases, I suggested it might be more cost-effective for those potential clients to consider hiring an attorney whose office was more local. The reason behind my suggestion was that, they would have the added expense of paying for my travel time to those locations whenever there was a hearing.

Am I entitled to a court-appointed attorney?

Not unless there are special circumstances. Court-appointed attorneys are generally only available in situations where you cannot afford an attorney and:

- The government is bringing a case against you or
- You could be incarcerated
- You do not, often, see court-appointed attorneys in divorce cases. However, you may, on occasion, see them in cases involving:
- Enforcement of child support or
- Child Protective Services cases

What do I do if I cannot afford an attorney?

I discuss this question in greater detail in the following chapter.

In Harris County and other counties, you may be able to find a program that can offer help if you meet certain income requirements.

There are often long waiting lists for these programs.

CHAPTER 4

THE DIRTY TRICK OF THE AMICABLE DIVORCE

Many people are reluctant to use a lawyer in a divorce because they think their situation is too simple or easy to justify paying for a divorce lawyer to provide help and guidance.

The same people think that, in order, to keep things "amicable" or as long as things are "amicable," they should avoid getting an attorney.

What many potential clients do not realize is that they are being "penny wise and pound foolish." Some of the most expensive and costly mistakes I see are when a lawyer does not represent someone.

For this reason, I am including an update of an article I wrote in September of 2017. I feel compelled to do so based on a recent consult.

The following stories are examples of some dirty tricks that have been played intentionally or accidentally on unwary and unprepared individuals who were seeking an amicable divorce. They demonstrate the high cost and consequences for simple mistakes that could have been easily avoided had the people I met been represented by a lawyer before the divorce.

If you do not bring it up, you might not be able to do so later
The lady with whom I consulted that inspired this update had a very sad story involving domestic violence. She wanted to be able to move away from her abuser.

However, in her divorce decree, there is a geographical restriction that forces her to live near her abuser because of the children they have together. When I learned that her husband went to court to finalize the case, I was hopeful because there might be time to undo what had happened.

However, when I looked up the case and saw when the judge had signed the order, I saw she had missed the deadline to file a motion to reopen the case.

I then had to spend an hour explaining to this woman how she is stuck living near her abuser, even though her ex-husband:

- Had choked her
- Had a family violence case pending against him
- Had hit her on multiple occasions
- Was not exercising his visitation

Res Judicata
The legal reason for this is because of "res judicata." This means a matter has been adjudicated by a competent court and may not be pursued further by the same parties.

All the facts that could have helped her before the judge signed the order, in most circumstances, cannot be brought up to change the order that was signed. The court only cares about new facts that occur after the judge signs the order.

The Danger of Playing Too Nice
Unfortunately, in her case, she was not represented by an attorney. She did not want to anger her husband by getting an attorney. She thought that if she played it nice, she could get the divorce and move away afterwards.

Another problem in her case was that she signed and cooperated with everything including:

- Signing a waiver
- Signing the final decree
- Going to court

She did not leave herself any wiggle room for undoing the divorce decree.

There is Still Hope
I did let her know that should some more bad facts occur, she could ask the court to modify the current order regarding the children. I also let her know another possible reason to modify is if her ex-husband continues not to exercise his visitation.

Unfortunately, the lady I met with did not find much comfort in what I told her because it did not provide any immediate help to her and only serves as a cautionary tale for others.

WAIVER OF SERVICE—MEANS YOU DO NOT HAVE TO BE SERVED

Personal service is not the only way to bring a party to a case under the power of the court so that the court can make orders regarding those individuals.

Alternatively, a person can waive their right to be personally served with a copy of the lawsuit by signing a waiver of service. The waiver of service must be signed in the presence of a notary, notarized, and then filed with the court.

It says you do not want to be served by a process server or constable/sheriff or by certified mail sent by the District Clerk.

Recently, I met with a father and his new girlfriend who were confused about why his paycheck was being garnished for child support. He told me that he barely made minimum wage and the amount of money he was being required to pay was more than he made at his job.

The other sad thing was that it had only been a few months since the order was signed and he was already in the hole several thousand dollars because what he earned was not covering what he was supposed to pay in child support.

The father told me that he had never been served. My first thought was that maybe he had been served by some alternative means, which meant the case could more than likely be reopened.

The father had obtained a copy of the order against him, and so I was able to read it. What I observed was:

- No one involved in the case had used a lawyer
- The paperwork said that the father had signed a waiver
- The paperwork said that the father had agreed and signed the order

I asked the father to excuse me, so I could go look up the case online. I went back to my office and looked up the case. Sure enough, the record showed that there was a waiver on file. I then looked at the order again and flipped to the signature page and it looked like the father had signed the order.

I then went back and explained what I had looked up and showed him a printout showing the waiver of service and his signature on the order.

I explained that he did not need to be served because the court record showed he had waived service and agreed to the order. However, if that was not the case, we could file paperwork and subpoena the notary regarding his signature.

His girlfriend then turned to him and asked if he had signed the paperwork. His response was that he did not know. In my book, that is the wrong answer to that sort of question. I explained his options for fixing the order.

As I saw it, either:

- He had signed the order and did not bother reading what he had signed
- The mother filled in the blanks after he had signed the order or
- The mother somehow convinced a notary to sign the documents saying the father had signed the waiver

In every option I gave him, it was going to cost him several thousand dollars—a lot more than it would have cost to hire a lawyer to get it done correctly the first time.

BEWARE OF STANDARD FORMS

That same day, I met with another unfortunate individual who should have hired an attorney. In her situation, she and her husband had been able to resolve the case amicably outside of court through mediation.

In the agreement, she and her husband were supposed to split his retirement account 50/50 using QDRO. The purpose of her consult was to find out how much my office would charge for drafting that document.

She had brought all the paperwork with her so I could review it. Once I saw the paperwork, I grew immediately concerned. She had:

- A <u>Mediation Settlement Agreement</u> (MSA) and
- A <u>Final Divorce Decree</u>

My concern was the divorce decree. It was not anything drafted by a lawyer. It was a standard form put out by a popular website. One of the warnings on the form is NOT to use it to divide a retirement account and to hire an attorney instead to draft the decree when you are trying to divide a retirement account.

When I reviewed the Final Divorce Decree, my suspicions were confirmed. The Final Divorce Decree did not divide the husband's retirement account but instead gave him 100% of the account. When I explained this to the wife, she was understandably upset. She thought she was hiring my office to help her with a closing document to divide up the retirement account only to find out the divorce decree that was supposed to reflect the Mediation Settlement Agreement said something quite different.

This was another instance where having a <u>divorce attorney</u> would have protected an individual. The divorce lawyer would have made sure that the Final Divorce Decree that was signed reflected the agreement and that her ex-did not accidentally or intentionally do anything sneaky.

KNOW WHAT FORMS TO USE AND THE CORRECT COURTROOM PROCEDURE

One husband I met with recently had managed to divorce his wife on his own without the help of an attorney. He accomplished this divorce by default. A <u>default divorce</u> means he divorced his wife:

- First by giving her notice and
- After he gave her notice, she ignored it

Once this happened, his wife was able to reopen the case by:

- Hiring an attorney
- Stating the husband did not use the correct forms
- Stating the husband did not use the correct procedure in the <u>divorce</u>

One of the things the husband had failed to do was file an inventory and appraisement with the court and explain to the correct party why his division of the property was a just and right division. Had the husband followed the correct procedure, his ex may not have been able to reopen the divorce.

CHAPTER 5

FORGET WHAT THE PAPERS SAY, I'LL DO THIS OR THAT

There are various manifestations of this dirty trick that I have seen where a spouse has asked the other spouse to ignore the language of the divorce decree and sign the papers. In this chapter, we will explore a few variations on this trick.

Child Support

One of the areas where I see this trick used most often is regarding child support. Below are a few examples of this trick.

- **No Job or Lost Job**—I'm sorry you lost your job; we do not need to change the order because I agree you do not have to pay me while you're unemployed.
- **Refund you The Money**—sign the paperwork that says X amount will be withheld from your paycheck for child support. I know it is too high, but I will give you back the difference.

- **I will Stop Child Support**—While you are taking care of the child, I will call the child support office and stop child support.
- **Pay Me Directly**—It takes too long for the child support order to send me the money. Just pay me the child support directly; it is easier and quicker that way.
- **A Lesser Amount than Guideline Child Support**—Let's put less in child support because I will help you with extracurriculars for the kids or daycare expenses.

Where Child Support is Owed
Inevitably in all these situations, the spouse who fell for one of those tricks will be surprised when he is served with enforcement paperwork that says he owe tens of thousands in arrears and faces possible jail time.

Lesser Amount than Guideline Child Support
I have heard about promises to "help out" with:

- Splitting Extracurricular Activity Expenses for the Kids
- Buying Diapers
- Buying Formula
- School Supplies
- Daycare

Those promises remind me of the quote by Cogsworth from the Disney Movie *Beauty and the Beast*, "Well, there's the usual things. Flowers, chocolates, promises you don't intend to keep."

Inevitably, the parent who said they would "help out" with things other than child support inevitably does not. When a potential consult asks me about accepting such a deal, I tell them they should get the money then they can buy those things for themselves.

Alternatively, those promises need to be put into the order as additional child support so that those promises are enforceable.

The Order is the Order Until the Judge Signs a New Order

Some parents assume:

- That child support automatically stops if one parent calls the child support office and asks for it to be stopped. However, that is not the case.
- It is too much hassle to change paperwork, and so it is not a big deal to make some verbal or written agreement outside of the order.

Something I tell parents who hire or consult with us is that, "the Order is the Order until a judge signs a new Order." This means that, until a parent petitions to modify the existing child support order and a judge signs a new order, the parent will continue to be liable under the existing order.

This means:

- If you do not pay the amount of child support specified in the order, because you lost your job and are no longer able to, you could get in trouble.
- If your spouse does not reimburse you the difference, they are not going to get into trouble.

- Your ex-spouse cannot just call the child support office and cancel child support (a judge is required to sign a new order)
- If you pay your spouse directly and do not keep track every payment, they could potentially tell the child support office you have never paid them, and you could be in trouble. I have seen this happen multiple times. Recently a dad told me he had never missed a payment, but because he paid her directly, he was having to try and produce proof for ten years of direct payments.

Child Custody and Visitation

Some of the tricks I have seen used when custody is involved include:

- **You can see the kids as much as you want**—"Sign the papers giving me sole physical custody. You know I will let you see the kids whenever you want."
- **We can take turns on custody**—"Give me custody this year, and then I will let you have custody when the child starts school (or substitute some such future event or time frame)."

Visitation

When it comes to visitation, it is true that you and your ex-spouse can deviate from the order as long as you both agree. However, if you ever get into an argument, you may be stuck with the standard visitation order in the order or worse yet, no visitation.

Child Custody

If you give up custody in the custody settlement order, you are probably stuck with not having custody unless your ex-spouse messes up.

This is because to change a custody order in Texas, you will need a "material and substantial" change in circumstances for either party or any child since the last order was signed. A court will want to know why it should flip custody and "it's my turn" is not a legally recognized reason.

If your child is doing well with your ex-spouse, a court is not going to want to rock the boat.

Property Division

Sometimes the dirty tricks I see involve property division.

One ex-wife I met with told me that she and her ex-husband had an agreement that he could keep the house in the divorce, but if he ever sold it, they would split the proceeds. She was upset because her ex-husband had just sold the house and told her that he was not going to give her anything.

I looked at the paperwork, and it clearly state that he got the house and there was nothing in the divorce decree regarding her getting any of the proceeds if the husband sold the house. I asked her about the agreement. She told me that it was a verbal agreement that she had had with her husband.

I had to break the bad news to her that a verbal agreement was probably unenforceable.

Moral of The Story
Remember, "the court order" is always controlling. Your verbal side-agreements are generally unenforceable.

At times, we have been able to help our clients with their side agreements, but it often means they have had to spend thousands of dollars and months or years of their lives for us to do so.

CHAPTER 6

EMBARRASSING YOUR SPOUSE DURING A DIVORCE

This chapter is inspired by some cases and consults I have had where a spouse has gone out of their way to try and embarrass their spouse.

This is done for a variety of reasons:

- Anger
- To teach their ex a lesson
- To try and achieve a strategic advantage

To prepare our readers for what they might expect during the divorce process, we will explore the various ways some spouses have tried to embarrass their soon-to-be ex. We will also discuss some things you should consider before you go down that path.

Serving Your Spouse in an Embarrassing Place

Serving divorce papers at work is perhaps the most commonly employed way that some spouses embarrass their ex. This one may be done either intentionally or out of necessity.

One reason this may be done (other than for malice) is that serving them at work or some other embarrassing place may be the only way to get a spouse served because the spouse is trying to avoid service or will not let anyone know where they are currently living.

However, some of my clients have sworn that it was done intentionally only to embarrass them. Often in these cases, they were still living in the same home, so there was no reason why it could not have been done at the house rather than while they were at work.

Recently one of my co-workers was telling me how her husband's brother had been served. I thought under the circumstances it was in very bad taste. The brother had been in a car accident and was in the hospital. The process server showed up and laid the paperwork on him while he was lying in bed and told him he had been served.

Something to keep in mind is that although there may be satisfaction in such gestures, at some point in the future, you may find that your spouse will retaliate and find a way to embarrass you. This can lead to your divorce turning into a very expensive, long, and embarrassing divorce.

Revealing Personal Information to Friends and Family

In one of our divorce cases, we represented a wife who was accused of adultery. In that case, the only evidence the husband had of the adultery were some very graphic emails and online chat sessions.

Our readers will know that Texas upholds the literal definition of adultery. Thus, graphic emails and chats might be considered cheating, but those alone would not meet the legal definition of adultery. Depending on the content, they might be evidence that adultery has taken place.

For revenge, the husband, in that case, let family members and friends know about the emails and chats.

Perhaps a more famous example of this would be when Tiger Woods' wife released a bunch of his text messages showing that her husband had been having affairs.

Unlike in Tiger Woods' case, your text messages, chats, or emails are unlikely to land you on late night talk shows or celebrity gossip sites.

However, you should keep in mind that just like in these two cases, your communications may eventually become part of a divorce or family law case, or perhaps may be revealed to friends or family in an act of spite by your ex.

Confronting the Paramore

Two of our law firm's most popular blog topics are "Can I sue the mistress?" and "Is adultery against the law?" It should not be surprising that I often get asked about confronting the mistress.

This confrontation takes various forms:

- Calling
- Showing up at the residence of the mistress
- Subpoena the mistress to appear in court as a witness
- Deposing the mistress

The motivations for doing any of the above varies. If there is a lot of property at stake, proving adultery would be a reason to ask for a disproportionate share of the property.

When there is not a lot of property at stake, then the motive is more likely revenge by embarrassing the mistress or the spouse. You may not be able to undo the fact that your spouse has cheated on you, but you can force them and the mistress to:

- Appear in court and answer embarrassing questions or
- Sit in a room with your attorney and answer embarrassing questions

Revenge Porn

Revenge porn is another way a divorcing spouse can embarrass their ex. Revenge porn occurs when:

- Someone obtains intimate pictures or videos of a person during a personal relationship, and

- Posts the pictures online after the relationship ends.

Many victims of revenge porn reported being threatened, harassed, stalked, fired from jobs, or being forced to change schools.

In its earliest stages, there was not a great legal remedy for these victims. In response to the problem in 2015, the Texas Legislature passed new statutes relating to revenge porn.

To my knowledge, none of my clients have been threatened with revenge porn. However, revenge porn was an issue in at least one of my cases. Our office represented a husband and father against the wife and mother.

In this case, she had filmed her encounters with her boyfriend who also happened to be married. Things must not have worked out between the two because she threatened to not only send the film to his wife but also to the school where he worked if he did not pay her off. Her boyfriend ended up paying the money, and she sent the film anyway.

She then discovered that what she had done violated several Texas laws, two of which are discussed below. When she was charged, the case made the news. She also ended up losing custody in court.

Under Texas Penal Code section 21.16.

A person commits the offense of "unlawful disclosure or promotion of intimate visual material" by disclosing, threatening to disclose, or promoting what is commonly referred to as "revenge porn."

A person commits an offense by disclosing revenge porn if:

- Without the effective consent of the depicted person, the person intentionally discloses visual material depicting another person with the person's intimate parts exposed or engaged in sexual conduct;
- The visual material was obtained by the person or created under circumstances, in which the depicted person had a reasonable expectation that the visual material would remain private;
- The disclosure of the visual material causes harm to the depicted person; and
- The disclosure of the visual material reveals the identity of the depicted person in any manner.

A person commits an offense by threatening to disclose revenge porn if the person intentionally threatens to disclose, without the consent of the depicted person, visual material depicting another person with the person's intimate parts exposed or engaged in sexual conduct and the actor makes the threat to obtain a benefit:

- in return for not making the disclosure; or
- in connection with the threatened disclosure.

A person can also commit an offense by promoting revenge porn if, knowing the character and content of the visual material, the person promotes the visual material on an Internet website or another forum for publication that is owned or operated by the person.

Civil Cause of Action—CPRC Ch. 98B

Not only did the legislature make revenge porn punishable as a crime, but it also created a civil cause of action. In 2015, the Texas Legislature also created a cause of action for victims of revenge porn.

This means the person who posted the video:

- Can be sued for financial damages by the victim and
- Can be held criminally responsible for their behavior

A defendant is liable to a person depicted in intimate visual material for damages arising from the disclosure of the material if:

- The defendant discloses the intimate visual material without the effective consent of the depicted person;
- The intimate visual material was obtained by the defendant or created under circumstances, in which the depicted person had a reasonable expectation that the material would remain private;
- The disclosure of the intimate visual material causes harm to the depicted person; and
- The disclosure of the intimate visual material reveals the identity of the depicted person in any manner.

A defendant is liable to a person depicted in intimate visual material for damages arising from the promotion of the material if knowing the character and content of the material; the defendant promotes intimate visual material...on an Internet website or another forum for publication that is owned or operated by the defendant.

A plaintiff can sue for actual damages, mental anguish damages, attorney's fees, and exemplary damages. A court can also grant injunctions against the disclosure or promotion, and the code provides for statutory damages of $500-$1,000.

Online Impersonation

Understandably, people going through a divorce are not always at their best. People going through a divorce will often say or do things that are hurtful because of the roaring emotions at play. Another way people can get themselves in trouble is an online impersonation.

One instance where this may have taken place made the news on June 25, 2015, when ex Galveston Judge Chris Dupuy was arrested for creating fake escort ads that purported to be posted by his former girlfriend.

The ads featured the women's photos and made clear that at least one of them was "VERY FETISH FRIENDLY." These ads were traced back to Chris Dupuy, who was charged with two counts of online impersonation.

He then spent 11 months in a Galveston County jail awaiting trial, after which a Galveston County District Court judge tossed out the charges, calling the statute used overbroad.

Texas Penal Code 33.07 was a relatively new statute passed by the legislature in 2009. This statute is often known as the cyber-stalking statute.

Under Texas Penal Code 33.07. ONLINE IMPERSONATION

(a) A person commits an offense if the person, without obtaining the other person's consent and with the intent to harm, defraud, intimidate, or threaten any person, uses the name or persona of another person to:

- create a web page on a commercial social networking site or other Internet website; or
- post or send one or more messages on or through a commercial social networking site or other Internet website, other than on or through an electronic mail program or message board program.

(b) A person commits an offense if the person sends an electronic mail, instant message, text message, or similar communication that references a name, domain address, phone number, or other item of identifying information belonging to any person:

- without obtaining the other person's consent;
- with the intent to cause a recipient of the communication to reasonably believe that the other person authorized or transmitted the communication; and
- with the intent to harm or defraud any person.

(c) An offense under Subsection (a) is a felony of the third degree. An offense under Subsection (b) is a Class A misdemeanor, except that the offense is a felony of the third degree if the actor commits the offense with the intent to solicit a response by emergency personnel.

CHAPTER 7

GETTING YOUR SPOUSE TO LEAVE THE MARITAL HOME

This chapter is inspired by some cases and consults I have had where a spouse has gone out of their way to get their spouse to leave the marital home.

Many of the consults I meet with have a lot of concern regarding whether it is a good idea to either continue to live in the marital home or to leave. While there is no "one size fits all" piece of advice that can apply equally to all inquiring spouses, there are some factors that are worth consideration across the board.

To prepare our readers for what they might expect, we will explore the various ways some spouses have tried to trick their spouse into leaving the marital home. We will also discuss some things you should consider before you agree to leave the marital home.

Temporary Restraining Orders Used to Trick Spouses into Leaving the Marital Home

I have represented multiple spouses who, after being served with divorce papers that included a TRO, thought they had to leave the marital home. This is because when they were served with the paperwork, they did not understand what the TRO means.

Often, their spouse wanted them out of the marital home and helped their misunderstanding by telling them that a TRO meant they have been instructed to leave the home, and if they do not leave and the police are called, they would be arrested.

Changing the Locks on the Marital Home

Another tactic I have seen used is changing the locks on the marital home and telling the spouse they are not allowed in the home. This has come up recently in two different consults.

Consult #1

In the first consult, the wife had changed the locks and told the husband to not come home. She had all his financial documents and his driver's license. The man wanted to know what he could do about it.

After talking with him, I found he owned the home, and his name was on the deed. I told him he could either:

- call a locksmith to help him get into the home, or
- he could let himself in even if he had to take a brick and break a window

The husband was concerned with his wife calling the police on him. I told the man even if she does, it is not against the law to break into your own home.

Bring a Witness / Or Record Everything on Your Phone
If she calls the police, I told him not worry about it. Remain calm and tell the police what was going on. If the man wants to be cautious, it would not hurt to have a friend come with him who could witness everything.

If he is unable to bring a witness, he could pull out his phone and record everything. If he takes one of these precautions, it will make it difficult for his wife to make up a story that the husband attacked her or threatened her.

Consult #2
In the second consult, the reverse had happened. The husband had changed the locks on the apartment, and the husband would not let the wife back into the apartment or let her get her things. I asked the wife whose name was on the lease.

The wife informed me that only her husband was on the lease. It was the same apartment complex, but they had recently changed apartments, and when that happened, her name never made it onto the new lease.

This made things a little more challenging because she probably would not get any help from the apartment manager for helping her get into the apartment. I suggested calling the police to at least come out because

- they may be able to help her get into the apartment by talking to her husband
- or failing that may be able to help her get her things.

Depending on the police officer, they may not want to get involved and tell the wife she needed to hire an attorney.

If that is the case, the wife has the option of either filing for:

- **Writ of Reentry**—through the Justice of the Peace or
- **Temporary Orders**—through family court

Do I have to move out because my spouse tells me to?

- No, you do not have to leave the home if your name is on the lease or mortgage.
- You do not have to move out just because your spouse tells you that he/she wants you to leave.
- Both parties have a right to stay in the home. No one can force you to leave your residence without a court order unless there is domestic violence.
- To get such a court order in a divorce, a temporary orders hearing must be held. During a temporary orders hearing, the judge will determine who is awarded the exclusive use of the home. This means that if you and your spouse cannot agree as to who will live where while the divorce is pending, the judge will make a temporary decision for you.
- In some cases, when there are spare bedrooms, the spouses may agree to live together until the divorce is finalized to save money and ease the transition for the children. For other families, continuing to live together

causes too much stress. The decision to move out is one that should be considered carefully and discussed with a caring family law attorney who can help you make the best decision for you and your family.

Alternative Scenarios Where the Answer Is Not as Clear
- If the marital home is owned by a spouse's parents and there is no lease agreement. However, they would need to go through an eviction process first.
- If you are common law married and the spouse owned the property before the marriage. I had a case where this was the situation, and the husband was able to file for eviction while the divorce was going on and get his spouse removed from the home. Again, the husband had to go through a hearing before removing his spouse.

Keep Your Children in Mind During the Divorce

A priority consideration in deciding whether a spouse needs to leave the home, or not, is if there are children involved. What is in their best interest must be taken, into account. If your position is that your children need to continue to live in the home—and with you as a result—then it may be in your best interest to request that you be given exclusive use of the home.

This is, also, important strategically because what occurs at the beginning and middle of a divorce, such as whether, you remain in the home, or not, and your spouse lives elsewhere, is what tends to end up happening ultimately.

Temporary Orders

In the timeline of a case, a temporary orders hearing is the first opportunity for both parties to appear before, the judge, that can potentially decide their fate, post-divorce. Thus, the question of whether a spouse leaves or does not leave the home prior to the temporary orders hearing must be considered very carefully. If your spouse does move out- and your kids remain with you, that is a huge hurdle for your spouse to overcome in the hearing.

Simply put, since your spouse has moved out, it looks like he (or she) is willing to leave the children behind and that is something that a judge will most likely not look highly upon. This alone can cause a judge to name you the "primary" joint managing conservator which allows you to choose the residence of the children in addition to having the exclusive use of the home.

Finalizing the Divorce

As a case moves towards its conclusion, the fact that you have remained in the house and your spouse has not, can cause a judge to more strongly consider awarding the home to you in a trial setting. Should you and your spouse settle the case before a final trial, then it will still give you such a strategic advantage that many opposing parties will not risk going to trial.

The reason being that the presumption is so strong that the party that has vacated the home will not be awarded the home in the trial, most people in this scenario will not want to wager additional time, energy, and attorney's fees to find out if they can overcome those odds.

Other Considerations

Other factors are important to consider as well when weighing whether to ask your spouse to move out of the home. There are emotional ties that each person living in a house will have that go beyond the structure itself. Memories and nostalgia, even if recent times have been bad, will cause most people to fight hard to remain in the house even if you kindly ask them to leave.

CHAPTER 8

TRIAL SEPARATION

Although this trick has its own chapter, in many ways, it is a continuation of the previous chapter regarding "Getting Your Spouse to Leave the Marital Home."

I have seen many spouses use the hope of reconciliation to get their soon-to-be ex-spouse to take all sorts of detrimental actions and jump through all kinds of hoops. Below I will give some examples of this trick in action.

Story #1—Getting Husband to Leave the Home

One gentleman I met with told me that his wife told him she still loved him but needed some space while they worked things out. If he did not give her some space, she would file for divorce immediately. This husband said he loved her and would do whatever it took to save his marriage.

So, he moved out of the home and went to stay with a friend for what he thought was going to be a short while.

Several months later, his wife served him with an Original Petition for Divorce. She was asking for sole custody of the children and exclusive use of the marital home.

The Moral of the Story

It would have been a good idea for the gentleman to have first consulted with an attorney before moving out of the marital home for a trial separation. He could have discussed with a family law attorney a way to arrange a trial separation in a way to protect his rights and not hurt his case should he end up in a divorce.

Story #2—Wife Moves to Dallas

Recently I met with a husband who had just been served with a Protective Order. He was confused because what his wife *was telling him* and what *was in the paperwork,* were completely different.

His wife was telling him that:

- She wanted to stay married to him
- She needed some time to think
- The paperwork, with which, he had just been served, just meant they were going to meditate and figure out things with the kids
- I let him know that according to the paperwork with which he had been served, none of what he had been told sounded true. The paperwork stated that he had committed family violence against his wife. If granted, the protective order:

- Would give the wife an increased chance of getting custody
- Would give her an increased chance of alimony
- Would mean he would not be allowed within 200 feet of her residence
- Would say he was not allowed within 200 feet of her place of employment
- Depending on what he did for a living, may mean he would lose his job
- He would no longer be able to possess a gun

Understandably, this gentleman was extremely upset by what he had learned. I also found out that his wife had moved to Dallas with the kids. I let him know that I would not be surprised if as soon as she met the residency requirements of Dallas, he may also soon be served with divorce paperwork as well.

I asked him what he wanted to do. The man let me know that he still wanted to be married to the wife. I let him know he could still be married to his wife if the Protective Order was granted. However, it would make his marriage more challenging if he and his wife could not live together.

I also let him know I judge people by what they do and not what they say. From what I saw, his wife's actions were telling him what she wants even if she was saying something else to him.

Moral of the Story

A protective order is a very serious lawsuit and needs to be dealt with right away. If it is granted, not only would there be immediate consequences to this husband, but it could also have implications in a potential divorce or custody case that might follow the protective order case.

The trial separation trick is effective because it takes advantage of the of the spouse's feelings and keeps them off balance and uncertain which allows the spouse to play the trick to take actions and get things accomplished, that they might otherwise not be able to do if their spouse was more proactive early in the divorce.

If the case was heading to a divorce as I suspected, the husband needed to act right away and file his case first. Otherwise, instead of being able to fight the case in Houston, he would have to fight the case in Dallas where she was currently living.

Additionally, if he filed the case in Houston now, there would be an increased chance of his wife being forced to move back to Houston with the kids, which would mean he would be able to more easily remain involved in his children's lives.

CHAPTER 9

STEPS BEFORE MOVING OUT OF THE MARITAL RESIDENCE DURING A DIVORCE

This chapter is a continuation of the discussion of the previous chapter. Sometimes I get questions from clients and potential clients who do not want to remain in the home. However, they have concerns that it may hurt them legally if they leave home.

Everyone involved in a case is different and has their own unique facts, but the following are some things you may want to consider and do before making your decision about moving out.

Step 1: Do not move out unless it is necessary

If there has been domestic violence, safety must be the highest priority and everything else a distant second. In other situations, though, the leaving spouse must recognize that moving out will have ramifications for the whole family—financially, legally, and emotionally.

Increased Financial Stress

Living together is a more cost-effective financial arrangement than when spouses separate. When adults and children live together under one roof, resources are pooled to provide the necessities of food and shelter, as well as luxuries like cable television and internet access. For example, while there may be five televisions in one house, they all can share one cable connection.

Once a spouse leaves home, resources are no longer pooled, and costs are doubled. There are now two mortgages, two electric bills, and two grocery bills. In families with children, moving out also means additional transportation costs as the children are transported back and forth between homes. Parents must also now furnish two different rooms for the children. The cost of living can easily double.

Step 2: Figure out the finances

An important step to take before leaving the marital home is to understand the family's finances. This means gathering documents related to income such as bank statements, tax returns, pay stubs, bills, and creating a budget.

Documenting Financial Information

The first step is to determine the total amount of income of both spouses. If one or both people work in salaried positions, this can be fairly, easy. However, figuring out how much is earned can be more difficult if one or both spouses are self-employed and have fluctuating incomes or have income that are not clearly documented.

Documenting is an important part of the divorce process. At a point in the future, you will be asked to prepare a financial information statement that will be used by a judge when making decisions regarding child support and spousal support. It is easier to access financial documents related to income and bills while both spouses still live together, so this should be done before leaving the marital residence. Once a spouse moves out, gaining access to important documents becomes more difficult.

Step 3: Prepare for parenting apart

Moving out can have a great effect on the children. Frequently, children are kept in the dark until the last possible moment. The leaving parent needs to comfort the children during the transition and help prepare them for a possible custody battle.

Help the Children Cope

A top priority for the leaving spouse, should be to minimize the stress put on the children. Many divorce courts in Harris and Montgomery County, Texas require both parents to attend a four-hour parenting class before a divorce is granted.

Child Custody and Visitation Journal

Many divorces result in a battle over custody of the children. Often in these battles, there are few documents or verifiable facts concerning the custody. A helpful tool in these cases can be a child custody and visitation journal.

A custody and visitation journal should contain documentation on each visitation—your notes on your child(ren), the other parent, exchanges, etc. Many divorce lawyers have found that the outcome of a custody or visitation case depends, in large part, on the preparation that goes into it. In this regard, there are many things you can do to aid in the preparation of your case.

In addition to tracking the pickup and drop-offs of your children in your custody journal, I would encourage you to write down important information and events as they happen, so you have a chronological diary.

You can write notes about:

- Late pick-ups and drop-offs.
- Missed or canceled visits.
- Health appointments and medical information.
- Discussions with the other parent.
- Your child's mood and emotions when interacting with the other parent.
- Your child's behavior.
- Issues you want to talk about with the other parent.
- How your child is doing in school and other activities.
- Your child's milestones and development.
- Anything you want to remember.

Time Chart

A time chart not only provides further evidences of the above-discussed information but also helps a divorce lawyer document how much time either parent is spending with the children.

This evidence (the journal/calendar/Time chart) can be used in court should custody become an issue.

Step 4: Itemize the property and the debt

When it's time to divide the property, having an accurate list of assets and debts, along with the documents that support the list, will be indispensable.

There are ways a divorce lawyer can gather this information after the leaving spouse has moved out, but it's slower, more expensive, and can be less reliable than gathering the information before leaving.

Assets

The leaving spouse should itemize all assets on a spreadsheet, detailing the date the asset was purchased, the purchase price, and the estimated current value. This can be straightforward for assets such as a house. Other assets will be more difficult to assess.

A divorce lawyer can provide you with a helpful form for this purpose. This form is later turned into what is called an inventory and appraisement for use in court or mediation.

Four categories of assets to consider:

- Marital residence and other real estate.
- Intangible assets, such as financial and retirement accounts, stocks, bonds, etc.
- Business interests.
- Physical assets, such as furniture, artwork, vehicles, etc.

Debts

The leaving spouse should also itemize debts on the spreadsheet, detailing the amount of principal owed, interest rate, creditor, and account numbers.

Five categories of debts to consider:

- Mortgages, equity loans, and other debts secured by real estate.
- Auto loans and other debts secured by physical assets.
- Credit cards, including store-specific cards and gas cards.
- Student loans.
- Tax liabilities.

Records

The leaving spouse should not only itemize the assets and debts but also photocopy as many supporting records and documents as possible.

Some of the records and documents to photocopy:

- Tax returns.
- Pay stubs.
- Statements for all financial and retirement accounts.
- Statements for all loans and credit cards.
- Vehicle titles.
- Photographs of physical assets, such as china, crystal, artwork, furniture, computers, etc.

The time spent photocopying supporting records and creating a thorough itemization will seem like an overwhelming task but can also be a tremendous advantage. The itemization will also prevent additional unscrupulous and unethical behavior on the part of the other spouse, and it will save money by reducing the work to be done by a lawyer who bills for his or her time.

Step 5: Gathering Resources

The leaving spouse must gather possible financial resources before leaving the marital home to avoid being disadvantaged during the divorce. The primary resource in divorce is money. Divorces are expensive and running low on money can put the leaving spouse at a strategic disadvantage, forcing him or her to make poor decisions.

If the leaving spouse is the main income provider in the family, this probably will not be the case. The main wage earner can control where their future paychecks are deposited and have the advantage of being in control of the main source of income. If the leaving spouse is not employed outside the home, amassing enough money to get through the divorce will be challenging.

The goal of gathering resources is to create and maintain a level playing field with the other spouse, not to leave him or her bereft. Judges take a dim view of a leaving spouse departing and leaving the other spouse destitute with no access to any money because all the bank accounts have been drained, credit cards canceled, or other such tactics.

Decisions about what and how much to take can have legal consequences and should be discussed with your lawyer to avoid making any damaging decisions.

Some resources to be gathered are:

- Earnings from paid employment.
- Furniture and children's toys and equipment.
- Available cash and liquid financial assets.
- Credit cards and lines of credit.

Even for someone with lots of disposable income, leaving the marital residence is not the time to increase one's standard of living. The leaving spouse should not make major purchases on expensive furniture, vacations, or vehicles. He or she should spend what is necessary and no more. Divorce puts a financial strain on everyone, and resources are best managed conservatively.

Step 6: Do Not Date

This step is simple to follow and frequently ignored. The leaving spouse should not engage in any dating activities. There is a multitude of legal reasons for this, all of which should be discussed with your lawyer. Until you are divorced, it is considered adultery and can affect the division of property in the divorce.

Step 7: Assemble the Team

After the leaving spouse has moved out, the situation can rapidly become stressful and difficult, so a leaving spouse will need trusted advisors to help him or her make the best decisions possible. Your lawyer will assist in creating a strategy for you during the divorce process. In some instances, it may also be appropriate to hire a private investigator or an accountant. Your lawyer can help the leaving spouse decide which of these team members are needed and help choose the right ones for your unique situation.

CHAPTER 10

SPOUSAL SPYING IN A DIVORCE

Our office has had to deal with cases where one party suspects their spouse, rightly or wrongly, of having an affair. They have seen signs: staying out late at night, giving vague information about their whereabouts, coming home later than usual or when their spouse is leaving for work, being secretive about their text messages. This often leads to a spouse trying to be a private investigator and gather information.

In today's world of technology, it is very easy for a spouse to become an amateur sleuth and bug telephone conversations, break into computers, and track where their soon-to-be ex is going.

In some of our articles, we have discussed the legality of spousal spying, as spying on a spouse may not just be offensive but illegal, and possibly a marital tort. Although it is legal in some circumstances, depending on the way it is done, when our client is contemplating doing such things, we caution them from engaging in activity that is reckless or illegal.

Why Would My Spouse Spy on me?

There may be several reasons why your spouse may be spying on you and these may include:

- To see if you are drinking or using drugs
- To see if you are having an affair
- Your spouse may be afraid you are gambling or have a spending problem
- Your spouse may think you are only pretending to go to work

You may also be leaving a relationship where your ex is abusive, controlling, and has little regard for what is legal.

The focus of this chapter will be to delve more into what is possible and the steps that can be taken to help protect you against legal and illegal spying by your ex.

Trying to get an Advantage in the Divorce

Your spouse may also be trying to get an advantage for the divorce.

Although it is no longer necessary to plead fault in a divorce in Texas, you can still state specific grounds under section 6 of the Texas Family Code for ending your marriage, including:

- Living apart
- Confinement in a mental hospital
- Cruelty
- Abandonment
- Conviction of a felony
- Adultery

A court may give more of the community property to the "innocent" spouse if the <u>fault is proven in divorce.</u>

How Can I tell if my Spouse is Spying on Me?

There are many ways your spouse may be spying on you in including:

- Monitoring your use of social media (such as Facebook)
- Cellphone tracking
- Recording or having you "bugged."
- Spyware—monitoring your mail, email, phone calls, and text messages
- Tracking you or your vehicle using EZ-Tag or GPS
- Watching you via video surveillance such as a "nanny cam."
- Having you followed by a private investigator
- Following you

Social Media Accounts

We have discussed this topic before. However, I bring it up again because you and your social media account can be your own worst enemy in a divorce.

Your social media account such as Facebook can be a goldmine for your spouse to know about:

- Where you are
- What you are doing
- Who you are hanging out with and
- Much more

Even if you unfriend your spouse and change the security settings on your account, that will not prevent someone with whom you are friends from supplying your ex with information.

Cell Phones

One of the first things you may need to do is get a new cell phone. If you are on a shared plan with your ex, it may be very easy for them to track your whereabouts. Many cell phone carriers make it easy for people sharing the same plan to stalk each other.

The Phone Bill

There is the obvious factor of being able to look at your bill and see who your spouse is calling and texting.

This was how a wife I met with told me she found out that her husband was hiring hookers. Her husband traveled a lot for work. She got a feeling he was unfaithful to her, so she decided to get online and look at the phone bill. She noticed a lot of weird calls/ text messages late at night.

The wife started calling the numbers, and they were all women. One woman she talked to confessed what she did. When she confronted her husband, he, at first, denied it but then when she told him what she had done, he admitted that he had been having sex with hookers.

AT&T—Parental Controls / Family Map

If you are on AT&T, the account owner can add things to the plan such as parental controls or family map.

With the family map, your spouse can know where you are, at any time. Your spouse can also block you from calling certain numbers or those numbers from being able to call you.

This happened in one of the cases that we handled. Our client was in a relationship with a very controlling husband. This husband kept her from being able to go anywhere without his permission.

He further isolated her by blocking her ability to call and speak with anyone, with whom, he did not approve, which included her parents.

Verizon—Parental Controls –Verizon Smart Family

Verizon's version of these same technologies is called Verizon Smart Family and Smart Family Premium which includes being able to view location.

The apps can be used to control who a family member is permitted to call or receive calls from and:

- Locate your family anytime
- Receive arrival and departure updates
- Get an estimate on how fast they are driving

Sprint—Family Plan

Sprint family locator can be used to:

- Get real-time interactive satellite maps with street addresses and landmarks for family members.
- Restrict phone use

Change your Passwords

You are going to want to change all your passwords. It is not going to help you if you get a new phone that is not on your spouse's plan if they can guess your password and still get into your account.

You will need to spend some time changing your passwords on ALL your accounts to something they will not be able to guess. Some important accounts to change your passwords on include:

- Phone carrier
- Bank and other Financial Accounts
- Apple / iPhone

iPhones & Other Smart Phones

I mention iPhones and Apple because there are larger concerns that include your spouse's ability to purchase movies or music and charging them to your iTunes account.

Find My iPhone

Apple devices are also set up so that you can use Apple's "Find My iPhone" feature.

This can be done by either getting online or downloading an app. This happened in a case where a wife took her daughter and ran away to a woman's shelter. The husband showed up and demanded to see his wife and daughter.

The people at the shelter tried telling him that they were not there. The husband made such a scene that the cops had to be called. The cops later found out that the way he tracked them was by using Apple's "Find My iPhone" feature.

Find Friends

Another thing you may want to check for is what apps are on your phone. There are various apps that can be downloaded on your phone to stalk you. Including an app that comes with most iPhones, "Find Friends."

Tape Recording your Spouse

We frequently get questions regarding the use of tape recorders or voice-activated recorders to catch their spouse. More and more, what we have been seeing are spouses who will use their phone to:

- Record their conversation with their spouse, using the phone as a tape recorder or
- Record their phone calls
- Take videos of their interactions with their spouse

In a case that closed not too long ago, a wife had recordings on her phone of the husband admitting to all kinds of behavior from drug use to misusing the marital finances.

In another case, the wife had managed to catch her husband hitting her on video using her cell phone.

The basic rule in Texas regarding recordings is that you can record any conversation in which you are a participant. This means you do not need your spouse's permission if you are taking part in the conversation.

Bugging your Spouse

The converse to the rule about being allowed to record conversations in which you are a participant is that you are not allowed to record a conversation where you are not a participant. This means it is illegal to bug your spouse to catch them talking to other people.

However, just because it is illegal does not mean that it does not happen. One spouse that we represented was convinced her husband was doing just that. He always seemed to know things that he should not know.

Eventually, she found all kinds of weird listening devices around her home.

Spyware

The recording devices do not even have to be a physical device. It can be your cell phone or computer. As mentioned earlier, various apps can be downloaded and used to stalk your location. There are also apps that can be used to:

- Monitor texting
- Monitor internet browsing
- Record phone calls
- Record location
- Track where pictures were taken
- Read emails

Most, if not all, of this would be illegal but is possible.

If you suspect that your spouse may be spying on you, it would be a good idea to get your cell phone and computer checked for spyware.

Watching you via Video Surveillance such as a "Nanny Cam."
Many families use nanny cams to monitor nannies, maids, or other domestic workers. However, sometimes in a divorce, it can be used to snoop on their spouse.

Many spouses give into the temptation to try and catch their spouse fooling around with a Paramore, and one tool they use is the nanny cam.

Are Nanny Cams Legal?
Yes, they are in Texas. However, you cannot:

- Record any conversation in which you are not a participant.
- You cannot record private areas of the home, such as a bathroom or bedroom.

This means you can only record in common areas and, in most circumstances, video without sound.

EZ-Tag and Other Electronic Toll Tags
Much like your phone, if you share an EZ-Tag or other electronic toll account with your spouse, you will want to get your own and remove your name from the shared account.

The EZ-Tag toll tag in the Houston area is a quick and easy way to pay for tolls. It also, however, lets someone know where you are at that exact moment and in which direction you are headed.

In most circumstances, this is not a big deal. However, this can be problematic if you are going through a contentious divorce or breakup. Two separate cases come to mind where the EZ-Tag was an issue.

Case #1—Stalking
In one case, a husband used the EZ-Tag to stalk his wife and figure out where she was going. He was convinced that she was cheating on him with her boss. Using the EZ-Tag, he was able to learn what part of town she was in and at what hours—which happened to be the same part of town her boss lived in.

Case #2—Running Up Tolls
In another case, the wife kept using the EZ-Tag to run up tolls. In that case, the husband did not want to know where the wife was going but it bugged him that she wouldn't stop using the EZ-Tag and he felt like she should be paying that bill.

OnStar and other GPS Navigation Systems
One of the best-known GPS navigation systems is OnStar. With OnStar, it can find out where your car is. This can be helpful:

- In a medical emergency, or
- If your car is stolen

As with the previous scenario, this can be problematic when your ex is using this tool to track your whereabouts. One of our clients had this problem. I suggested she take it to the dealer for help either disabling or removing it from her vehicle.

Tiwi system and other GPS Tracking Devices

Several simple devices are now on the market that allow you to track where, when, and even how fast someone is driving.

One example of this is the Tiwi, which is marketed to parents to be able to keep track of their teen drivers. It plugs into the car's vehicle diagnostics port. It may be a good idea to have your car thoroughly checked for such devices.

Locking your Credit Report

Another thing to consider is to lock your credit reports. Locking your credit is also known as a credit freeze. This is normally used as a tool that lets you restrict access to your credit report, which in turn makes it more difficult for identity thieves to open new accounts in your name.

We generally suggest this option to clients who are concerned their spouse may try and open accounts in their name. However, you might also want to consider putting a lock on your credit, so a less-than-ethical spouse cannot pull your credit to see what you have been doing.

This may not give an ex the same play by play information as having online access to your credit card or debit card. However, this issue came up recently and so it makes the list.

How Can I Protect Myself from Spousal Spying?

The internet and other technology have made surveillance by private individuals much easier for those who are willing to pay some money and put forth the effort. However, it is possible to take steps to make it more difficult for your spouse to spy on you even without knowledge of the technology your spouse may be using.

These steps include:

- Installing a firewall on your computer
- Password protection, and
- Encryption software

Firewall
A Firewall helps prevent unwanted access to your computer from the Internet.

Password Protection
Password protection is available on most email programs and websites including financial institutions.

One example would be two-step verification. Two-step verification is a process that involves two authentication methods. These are performed one after the other to verify that the person requesting access is who they are supposed to be.

This could be as simple as getting a text message with a code after you plug in your password. You would then plug in the code and have access to the account. Anyone who does not know your password and has your cell phone would not be able to access the account.

Encryption Software

Encryption software is one method of sending electronic messages in a format that prevents someone without "decrypting" software be able to read them.

CHAPTER 11

FAKE EMAILS AND
ELECTRONIC EVIDENCE

There is much discussion these days about "fake news." It appears that the term is popping up everywhere from talk show hosts, the White House, and TV dramas such as the "The Good Fight." The Term "Fake News" refers to fabricated news stories published by fake news websites that have no basis in fact but are presented as being factually accurate.

I mention this because just as we in society need to be careful of where we get our news, it is important as you proceed in your divorce to be careful of the emails and electronic evidence that can be used. Not only is it easier in today's world to fabricate the news, but it has also become easier to fabricate all kinds of electronic evidence such as:

- Phone calls
- Emails
- Text messages
- Social media accounts

- Photographs
- Medical records
- Doctors notes

Technology is changing every day at what feels like an ever-increasing speed. Technology has changed many aspects of society including family law. Technology now plays a role in every aspect of a case including:

- Before the case begins
- Discovery
- During the case and
- After the case has concluded

Technology can have both positive and negative effects on the outcome of any case. To prepare our readers for what to be on the lookout for, we will explore the various ways some spouses have tried to use fake evidence in their case.

Electronic Evidence Is Not Assumed to Be More or Less Reliable

Electronic evidence is not automatically assumed to be more reliable or less reliable, than traditional documentary evidence. Even before computers and other sources of electronic evidence, there has been a possibility of forgery or misleading editing of:

- Documents
- Letters, and
- Photos

All evidence may be faked. In Texas, a party introducing the evidence must make a threshold showing of admissibility.

Fake Doctor's Notes

In one of our cases, one of the big issues in the divorce case was that the wife was having a lot of difficulties getting their child to school on time.

During a temporary order hearing, it was brought to the judge's attention how many times the child had missed school or been tardy to school. As a result of all the absences/tardiness, there was a good chance the child would have to repeat a grade. The judge warned the wife that if the child had any more unexcused absences, custody would be switched from her to her husband.

The child continued to miss school. However, the wife was able to produce doctor's notes showing that the absences were excused. It later came out these notes were fabricated. The wife had a computer background and had used Adobe Photoshop to fabricate the doctor's notes.

When the doctor's records were subpoenaed, it showed the child had never been to the doctor on the days in question. The doctor also testified that he had never seen the child and was quite upset that his signature had been forged.

Fake Medical Records

It has not come up in any of our cases yet, but while I was researching this chapter, I came across a website called www. fakeababy.com. This website sells fake:

- Medical records
- Ultrasounds
- Pregnancy tests
- DNA tests

The company says that its purpose is novelty-only and has been responsive to discovery requests.

Fake Text Messages

According to *Family Lawyer Magazine*, text messages have become the most common form of divorce evidence. A recent survey by the American Academy of Matrimonial Lawyers (AAML) showed that social networking sites had become a hot source for evidence.

Text messages are sometimes admissible in Texas divorce courts. Some reasons a spouse may want to try and admit text messages may be to:

- Prove adultery
- Prove family violence
- Prove the best interest of child and impact custody

Something to be aware of is that there are cell phone apps available that can create fake text messages. These apps can be used to create the appearance of:

- Sending or receiving messages from anyone
- Sending photographs
- Creating the impression of a text failed to send

In 2014, the authenticity of text messages was an issue during Johnny Depp and Amber Heard divorce. The text message exchange in question, detailed an alleged assault. The policed declined to file charges in the case because there were no physical signs of abuse.

Fake Phone Calls

Just as there are apps out there that fabricate text messages and create the appearance of sending or receiving the message from anyone, there are apps that fool or "spoof" caller identification and make it appear that someone is calling from someone else's phone number.

Chances are even if you are not involved in a divorce, you may have received a phone call from someone hiding or faking or "spoofing" their phone number.

This is because telemarketers have increasingly been using this technique to make it look like the phone number they are calling from is a local phone number. This is called neighbor spoofing. I have a co-worker who says he got a call from a telemarketer who had spoofed his own phone number, so it looked like he was getting a call from himself.

In a divorce context, someone may want to spoof a phone number to falsify evidence that:

- Their spouse is making harassing phone calls
- Establish proof they are on a business trip
- Create evidence of adultery that one spouse is calling their "lover."

Another reason I have seen spouses spoof numbers (other than creating fake evidence) is to evade a blocked number. One spouse, for whatever reason, may have blocked their spouse's number from their phone. A tech-savvy spouse decides this isn't a problem because they will use an app to spoof someone else's number that isn't blocked.

This can be problematic if you are trying to show that your spouse is harassing you by making repeated phone calls. This is because all the numbers that you are being called from are different. However, this can be overcome by getting an app to record those phone calls so you can prove that it is your spouse calling you.

Fake Calls to 911 & Swatting

Swatting is a dangerous version of spoofing. It is where a person will call 9-1-1 from a spoofed number to report a phony dangerous situation such as a bomb threat at the house of the hoax's victim. SWAT teams will respond accordingly, leading to a potentially deadly situation for the victim. This would be a felony under the Texas Penal Code. Thankfully, this has not happened in any of my cases.

Fake Emails / Email Phishing

Spoofing usually occurs with telephone calls and text messages. However, email is another common source of spoofing. A sender may falsify the name and email address of the sender. Creating fake emails can serve the similar purpose of creating fake evidence.

However, another reason may be for what is known as "email phishing." Email phishing is a type of online scam where criminals send an email that appears to be from a legitimate company and asks you to provide sensitive information.

If you fall victim to an email phishing scheme from your spouse, they may be able to gain access to your email account, bank account, social media, or other online accounts.

2-Step Verification
One way to help protect against email phishing or hacking is to make sure your accounts are set up with 2-step verification.

Two-step verification is a process that involves two authentication methods performed one after the other to verify that the person requesting access is who they say they are.

For example, you try and log into your email from a computer you have never used before. After you enter your email address and password, if 2-step verification is set up, you would then get a text message with a code that you would need to enter. This is not perfect protection against phishing, but it does make it more difficult.

Fake Facebook or Social Media Accounts
We have been involved in more than one case where Facebook profiles have played a role. The AAML survey revealed that social networking sites had become a hot source of evidence. Over eighty percent of family law attorneys surveyed have been involved in a divorce where social media evidence has played a role.

In many of those cases, one party has wanted to use information from the other party's profile as evidence. In the cases where we have been involved, normally when a fake Facebook profile has played a role, it has been one party creating the fake profile to try and friend the other party to gain access to Facebook posts.

However, there have been occasions when one party has created a fake profile of their spouse then exchanged communications back and forth to incriminate their ex.

Save Electronic Communication
One way of combatting fake electronic evidence is to make sure that you save any electronic communication between yourself and the other party. If you do this, you will be able to show that the other party has fabricated something.

Learn Everything You Can About Different Types of Evidence
Many people, whether they are parties to a case or attorneys representing parties to a case, can be reluctant to deal with electronic evidence. However, it is important to learn and be comfortable working with all types of evidence that can be useful as evidence in a case including electronic evidence.

CHAPTER 12

HIDING ASSETS DURING YOUR TEXAS DIVORCE

This chapter is inspired by several consults I had over the last two days where the topic of asset hiding came up in the context of a divorce. Asset hiding is one of the most popular dirty tricks during a divorce.

The phrase *asset hiding* probably conjures up imagery from the movies in which spouses hide money in offshore accounts. While I am sure that happens, there are some more mundane yet effective tactics you should be on the lookout for.

Red Flags that Your Spouse May be Hiding Assets

- Clients are often concerned that their spouse may be hiding assets. Some red flags to look for include:
- Refusing to share financial information.
- Diverting mail
- Decrease in income
- Controlling behavior

Refusing to Share Financial Information

If your spouse does not share financial information with you such as how much money is in an investment or bank account, this could indicate they are hiding assets.

Diverting Mail

If your spouse starts sending mail to another location, this is another good indicator they are trying to hide something. This could include a secret bank account they do not want you to find out about.

Decrease in Income

If there is a sudden decrease in your spouse's income, this is another good indicator they are diverting money elsewhere. It is quite easy these days to set up direct deposit into multiple accounts. So, if your spouse is depositing less money into a joint account, this may mean there is other money going elsewhere.

If you notice any of the above signs or any other signs that set off alarm bells, you should consult with a Texas divorce lawyer. An experienced divorce lawyer will help you determine what your rights are and steps you can take to protect yourself.

Hiding Assets

Hiding assets can take many forms including:

- Hiding income
- Moving money to a family member or friend's account
- Hiding money in offshore accounts
- Overpaying taxes
- Hiding money in sneaky investments

- Undervaluing business interests

Hiding Income

In one consult, the individual had a second job where they were compensated largely in cash. They were bragging in the consult how their spouse had very little knowledge of how much money they made from this job and so it would be easy to hide that money from them.

I cautioned this individual that if it were discovered they were trying to hide assets, a judge could severely punish them during the divorce in various ways, which could include, awarding their spouse a disproportionate share of the marital property along with other sanctions.

One of the things a Texas divorce lawyer will be on the lookout for is a spouse trying to hide income. Our office has caught more than one spouse trying to understate their income. The last time this came up, they were self-employed and tried to say that they only made a certain amount of money a month. However, when we were able to obtain their bank statements, we saw that they were depositing ten times the amount they had said each month.

Moving Money to a Family Member or Friend's Account

In another consult, a husband asked me a couple of questions regarding hiding assets that are worth addressing for our readers. The questions were:

As an attorney, can you help me hide assets from my wife?

Can I move money into a family member or friend's account to hide money from my wife?

Can an Attorney Help Their Client Hide Money from Their Spouse?

Per the Texas Disciplinary Rules of Professional Conduct, Texas attorneys have an ethical duty to not "engage in conduct involving dishonesty, fraud, deceit, or misrepresentation."

A spouse has a similar duty to their ex. It is highly likely that at some point each spouse will be requested to swear an oath as to all the assets and debts they are aware of. If a spouse conceals information and their attorney learns of the truth, their attorney may be obligated to withdraw from representing this client in further proceedings.

Hiding the Money from Their Spouse in Another Person's Account?

As my answer to the question above implies, hiding money in another person's account is not permissible during a divorce. Before a divorce, there are no court orders that would prevent a spouse from engaging in that activity.

However, I also explained that one of the first things his wife's attorney will probably do during the divorce is to ask for two years' worth of bank statements to look for large sums of money being moved around.

If it is discovered that money has been moved, his wife could ask to be awarded 100% of the money that he tried to hide based on his fraud on the marital estate. This would also paint him in a very unfavorable light with the court and call into question the truth of everything he said or presented to the court.

Hiding Money in Offshore Accounts

Hiding money in a foreign country seems like something you might see in the movies or read about in a newspaper or magazine about some rich celebrity. However, this is a dirty trick you should still be aware of. One of the biggest problems associated with this dirty trick is that even if discovered, it can be very difficult to recover the money.

Foreign Accounts Easy to Open

In today's world of the internet and ease of travel, it is incredibly easy to set up foreign bank accounts. The foreign banks also often make accessing this money incredibly easy with ATM and debit cards. Often a spouse does not even consider that their spouse may be doing such a thing during a divorce as was the case an ex-wife I met with, not too long ago.

Within the last month, an ex-wife contacted our office regarding her suspicions that her former husband had hidden money in another country. Her husband had run into problems with the IRS and convinced her, that, to protect her, they should divorce. He also told her that he was giving her everything.

He later moved to a foreign country. A few years later, after the divorce, she found out that her ex-husband was back in the United States and had a very lavish lifestyle and was living in a manner that leads her to believe that her ex-husband had lied to her about the money they had during the marriage and probably had some hidden accounts.

What Can be Done?

This ex-wife wanted to know what could be done. I explained *post-divorce discovery* and the legal remedies that were available should we discover hidden assets. If fraud is discovered in a reasonable time, you can file a motion to set aside the Final Divorce Decree. Alternatively, if the period for filing such a motion has expired, a separate post-divorce lawsuit can be filed to divide up any undisclosed assets.

Something to keep in mind is that although a court may make an order that off-shore assets be divided between the spouses, it can be very difficult, time-consuming, and expensive to try and convince the foreign jurisdiction to obey a United States orders.

Although foreign accounts can be easy to open, they are becoming more difficult to hide. Due to concerns regarding terrorism, the United States and several foreign countries cooperate regarding reporting certain information to each other.

Many foreign banks will send the IRS information regarding United States citizens. This makes reviewing tax returns an important tool for trying to detect foreign bank accounts.

Be Careful

Another thing to consider when deciding if your spouse may have hidden money overseas is the financial resources of the marriage. If you and your spouse are living paycheck to paycheck and you have a good handle on where the money is going, then this is probably not a dirty trick your spouse is engaging in.

Unfortunately for the husband in one of my cases, his wife became convinced that her husband was hiding money offshore. In this case, the husband, though, was just scraping by as a music teacher. Nothing in the case would have indicated that he had engaged in this underhanded trick. The couple was severely underwater with a credit card and other debts. Despite this, she and her attorney went on a witch hunt with legal discovery to find the hidden assets and turned what should have been maybe a $3,500-$7,000 divorce into a $40,000 divorce.

Overpaying Taxes

In one case where I represented the wife, the husband had tried to hide marital money by overpaying on his federal income taxes. He had set it up with his employer where more money than necessary was being taken out of his paycheck for taxes.

During settlement negotiations in mediation, we had settled all issues except the spouses filing of taxes together and splitting any tax refund. When we suggested doing just that, the husband hit the roof and said no. We pressed the issue and said that we were willing to walk away from the agreement and proceed with going forward to trial.

After hearing that this case may be going to trial, the other side relented, and parties agreed to split any tax refund. We later found out what the husband had done and that the refund was $25,000.

Hiding Money in Sneaky Investments

Another tactic for trying to hide money is to place it in an investment vehicle the spouse may not suspect; one such investment vehicle is a children's 529 plan.

A 529 plan is supposed to be used to help families save money for their children's college education. These plans offer certain tax benefits as incentives to encourage parents to save.

A 529 plan is set up so that:

- The parent is the account owner and
- The child is named as beneficiary

However, 529 plan funds can be withdrawn at any time by the owner, usually with tax penalties. This freedom to withdraw makes them possible vehicles to hide money during a divorce.

One example of this would be to put money that normally would be divided during a divorce in a 529 and pretend that it is for the child to withdraw after the divorce. This would be much like the tactic described above of overpaying taxes, so you do not have to divide it with your spouse. You then get that money back after the divorce.

There was a concern in at least one of my cases that this tactic was being used. We solved the problem during our mediation by dividing up two similarly funded 529's between the two spouses, who were then made constructive trustees of the funds that were only to be used for the benefit of the child's education.

Under-Valuing Business Interests

For purposes of calculating child support, it is relatively easy to calculate when a person is an employee. However, as discussed above regarding hiding income, it can be more difficult when that individual is self-employed or an entrepreneur. This is because an entrepreneur can more easily manipulate things within a business to show less income.

During a Texas divorce involving business, the value of the business is often a major focus of the division of property. There are several different approaches to valuing a business. One dirty trick is to try and undervalue the business, so there is less to provide. If your spouse is in control of the business, they are in the best position to know what it is worth.

If you are not the spouse in control of the business, rather than rely on your spouse regarding the value of the business, you may want to hire an independent business appraiser who is accredited in business valuation to help you evaluate what the business is worth.

How Can I Find Out if my Spouse is Hiding Assets?

One way to help detect if your spouse is hiding assets is to conduct discovery. Discovery usually involves one or more of the following documents:

- Request for Disclosure
- Request for Production
- Written Interrogatories
- Requests for Admission
- Sworn Inventory and Appraisement
- Depositions

One of the unique and important forms of discovery in a Texas divorce is to require spouses to prepare and file a sworn inventory and appraisement of all marital assets and debts. This inventory and appraisement will itemize all financial accounts of the marriage.

Another helpful form of discovery is a request for production. This request forces the spouse to produce statements for financial accounts including bank statements and other written documentation.

It is often helpful to compare these statements to the inventory and appraisement. If this comparison raises questions or needs clarification, additional discovery can be conducted including a request for interrogatories that asks questions or to conduct a deposition of the spouse.

If more expertise is needed, an attorney can employ a forensic accountant to review the financial records in a divorce to try and detect anomalies, irregularities, or hidden assets.

CHAPTER 13

WASTING MARITAL ASSETS OR GOING ON A SPENDING SPREE

When a divorce is on the horizon, sometimes otherwise honest spouses start to act out of character. This can often take the form of going on a spending spree. This spending spree often leaves both spouses with more debt than they can usually afford by the time the divorce is over. This chapter will discuss how to recognize when a spouse is wasting assets and what can be done about it during your Texas divorce.

What is Wasting Assets in a Texas Divorce?
Wasting of assets can happen during a marriage or during a divorce. A spouse who wastes assets is one who squanders a couple's savings or racks up credit card debt either during the marriage or the divorce process.

A good faith, use of money, or investment that does not work out does not constitute wasting assets. However, misuse of community property resulting in losses may give rise to a claim of wasted assets. Some examples of wasteful spending may include:

- Gambling debts
- Expensive gifts to family members or friends
- Money spent on an extramarital affair or lover
- Extreme spending from a couple's joint account or credit cards
- A new loan that is taken out without the other spouse's knowledge or approval
- New car purchase
- Major business losses
- Significant stock investments.
- Getting elective surgeries
- Getting teeth fixed
- Fixing up and making significant improvements to separate property
- Using joint account money to pay down credit cards or other loans
- Buying household items that will be needed to set up a new residence post-divorce with joint credit cards or joint bank accounts

Fraud on the Community—Division and Disposition of Reconstituted Estate

Constructive fraud, waste, and breach of fiduciary duty all mean the same thing in the context of a divorce.

These claims can be asserted under family code during the divorce.

Does a spouse owe another spouse a fiduciary duty in Texas?
A fiduciary duty would mean they have a legal obligation to act in the best interest of another (the other spouse).

The Texas Supreme Court found that there is unquestionably a fiduciary relationship owed by the spouses to each other and the management of the community estate. (Schlueter v. Schlueter, 975 S.W.2d 584 [Tex. 1998])

Actual Fraud
To prove actual fraud, a spouse must show the other spouse transferred community property for the primary purpose of depriving the claimant of the property with dishonesty or an intent to deceive, which resulted in harm to the community estate.

The spouse alleging actual fraud has the burden of proof, which can be more difficult than constructive fraud because they have to prove their spouse acted dishonestly or with the intent to deceive.

Constructive Fraud
The argument for constructive fraud is generally that a spouse has breached their fiduciary duty to their spouse in some way. Thus, if a spouse is misappropriating marital funds or assets from the community estate, they are not acting in the best interest of the other spouse.

Constructive fraud transfers the burden of proof to the spouse who made the transfers to show the transfers were fair.

Factors a Texas divorce court will consider in determining whether there has been constructive include:

- The relationship between the spouse and the recipient;
- The size of the gift or transfer about the total size of the community estate;
- The adequacy of the estate remaining to support the other spouse in spite of the gift or the transfer; and

Any special justifying factors for the gift or transfer.

Section Texas Family Code Section 7.009 states that:
(a) In this section, "reconstituted estate" means the total value of the community estate that would exist if an actual or constructive fraud on the community had not occurred.

(b) If the trier of fact determines that a spouse has committed actual or constructive fraud on the community, the court shall:

- (1) calculate the value by which the community estate was depleted as a result of the fraud on the community and calculate the amount of the reconstituted estate; and
- (2) divide the value of the reconstituted estate between the parties in a manner the court deems just and right.

(c) In making a just and right division of the reconstituted estate under Section 7.001, the court may grant any legal or equitable relief necessary to accomplish a just and right division, including:

- (1) awarding to the wronged spouse an appropriate share of the community estate remaining after the actual or constructive fraud on the community;

- (2) awarding a money judgment in favor of the wronged spouse against the spouse who committed the actual or constructive fraud on the community; or
- (3) awarding to the wronged spouse both a money judgment and an appropriate share of the community estate.

This means if the waste is determined, the innocent spouse may have a claim for reimbursement.

What Happens if a Judge Determines My Spouse Wasted Assets?

If wasting of assets can be proven, a judge can consider that when deciding how to divide marital property, to ensure the innocent spouse is reimbursed. A judge has few options including:

- Awarding the wronged spouse an appropriate amount of the community property
- Awarding a money judgment in favor of the wrong spouse against the spouse who committed the wrong or
- both

Spousal Maintenance or Alimony

If a court determines that a spouse is entitled to post-divorce spousal maintenance or alimony, the court can also consider any fraud as a factor when determining an amount of spousal maintenance.

Texas Family Code Sec. 8.052 states:

A court that determines that a spouse is eligible to receive maintenance under this chapter shall determine the nature, amount, duration, and manner of periodic payments by considering all relevant factors, including:

- (6) acts by either spouse resulting in excessive or abnormal expenditures or destruction, concealment, or fraudulent disposition of community property, joint tenancy, or other property held in common.

CHAPTER 14

DAMAGING, DESTROYING, OR SELLING MARITAL ASSETS IN TEXAS

This section is inspired by one of the questions I frequently hear regarding damaging, destroying, or selling marital assets. The question takes on some of the following variations:

- Can I sell X property?
- Can my spouse sell X property?
- My spouse destroyed X; what can I do about it?
- My spouse damaged X property; what can I do about it?

Unfortunately, the answer, as in many legal questions, is that it depends. This chapter will explore how timing and different circumstances can affect the outcome.

Can my Spouse or I Sell our Property?
This is a question I get a lot when divorce is on the horizon. If nothing has been filed with the court, then there are no court

orders to prevent either you or your spouse from doing anything they want with the marital property.

The beginning stages of divorce are often one of the scariest times because of the lack of court orders. This is because there is a lot of uncertainty of your rights and your spouse's rights.

After Paperwork is Filed

Once the divorce paperwork has been filed, some counties in Texas have standing orders that go into effect and place rules on how money can be spent and on selling, damaging, or destroying property.

If the county does not have a standing order, you can ask the court for a temporary restraining order. This is very similar to a standing order, but it must be requested and is routinely granted by family law judges.

A temporary restraining order in Texas is not a protective order; this is a common misconception. Generally, a Texas temporary restraining order has more to do with maintaining the status quo (much like a standing order) and is generally not intended to keep an individual from being around another individual or location.

The big difference between a temporary restraining order and a standing order is that temporary restraining orders are only good for 14 days. If requested, temporary restraining orders can be renewed for an additional 14 days. The idea behind a temporary restraining order is that they will provide some temporary protection until there can be a hearing before a judge can make more permanent orders for the duration of the divorce.

How is Property Divided in Texas?

In general, Texas Community Property is property acquired by either spouse during the marriage.

There is a rebuttable presumption that all property owned during the time of marriage is community property.

One of the things I tell clients and potential clients regarding property division during a divorce is that from the minute they are married until the minute they are divorced, any property, debts, or income earned are potentially on the table for division during the divorce.

The exception to this is any property that can be proven to be separate property.

To rebut this presumption, spouses must provide clear and convincing evidence that an asset is separate property in Texas.

Separate Property in Texas is:
- Property acquired before marriage.
- Property acquired during marriage by gift, devise, or descent.
- Property acquired during marriage but purchased with separate property funds.

Family Heirlooms

Family heirlooms can probably be shown to be separate property. However, something to consider is that if they were gifted, such as Grandma's wedding ring to your bride, then it may no longer be your separate property; it may now be the separate property of your ex.

Wedding rings are a good example of being the separate property of the person they were given to and not normally subject to division in a divorce. However, there is some case law that might provide a little wiggle room regarding family heirlooms.

Other Ways to Prevent a Spouse from Destroying, Selling, or Damaging Marital Property?

The best remedy is prevention. One of my suggestions to clients and potential clients is to move any property they are concerned about to a safe location. Some of these items may include:

- Inherited items
- Photos
- Things of sentimental value
- Valuables in safe
- Financial documents
- Things that cannot easily be replaced

I tell my clients and potential clients these items will ultimately need to be disclosed in the inventory during the divorce. However, by moving them to a safe location, they can ensure they do not end up in the trash, a garage sale, or pawn shop. Unfortunately, not everyone behaves civilly during a divorce, and a bit of caution is often prudent.

If you do not remove or cannot remove the items to a safe location, you can at least:

- Inventory your valuables and create a list.
- Photograph the property and date the photographs.
- Locate any proof you may have of what was given to you, inherited, or owned before the marriage.

At least in this way, you have documented the condition of the property and you can prevent your spouse from saying the item never existed.

What if my Spouse has Already Destroyed, Damaged, or Sold Marital Property?

One remedy is to plead for marital waste. As we discussed previously, the Texas Supreme Court found that there is unquestionably a fiduciary relationship owed by the spouses to each other and the management of the community estate. (Schlueter v. Schlueter, 975 S.W.2d 584 [Tex. 1998])

If it can be shown that waste took place, the innocent spouse may have a claim for reimbursement.

If wasting of assets can be proven, a judge can consider that when deciding how to divide marital property, to ensure the innocent spouse is reimbursed. A judge has few options including:

- Awarding the wronged spouse an appropriate amount of the community property.
- Awarding a money judgment in favor of the wronged spouse against the spouse who committed the wrong.

- Or both options.

The downside of this remedy is that it will not help to replace things that cannot be replaced such as photos or inherited items.

CHAPTER 15

THE DIRTY TRICK OF STRIPPING THE HOUSE

This chapter is a continuation of the previous chapter regarding damaging, destroying, or selling marital assets. Some spouses move everything out of the house before they file for divorce. Alternatively, if a spouse moves out and leaves things behind, the remaining spouse takes the time to make everything that has been left in the house disappear.

This may feel great at the time but will make your spouse angry and generally leads to a more expensive divorce. Additionally, it can give your spouse reimbursement claims for the personal property you took. This may mean you end up with things you do not want and have less cash.

If you are the spouse that is a victim of this dirty trick, you may feel powerless while it is going on. You will probably be angry with your spouse, mad with your attorney, and frustrated with the legal system because you feel like your spouse is getting away with it.

This chapter will discuss a few examples of this trick in action and make suggestions on how to avoid the problem so, hopefully, you will not fall victim to this trick.

Example #1—Stripping the House Before Moving Out

In a recent case that I was part of, the wife sat down with her husband and explained that she wanted a divorce and it was time for him to move out. The wife felt that the husband took the information remarkably well.

She was scheduled to be out of town for a few days on a business trip and had arranged, for her parents to watch their daughter while she was gone. The moment her plane touched down, and she turned on her phone, she got a text message from her husband that he had:

- Hired an attorney
- He had full custody of their daughter

The wife understandably was distraught and, immediately, arranged a return flight. Her husband refused to take her calls other than to tell her to call his attorney.

When she made it to the house, she found that much of the house had been stripped of furniture and personal items. One of the hardest hit rooms was the daughter's bedroom; nothing was left in that room.

Talking to the husband's attorney did not help. His attorney called her names and got her to sign some documents that the wife should not have signed. The attorney used the wife's desperation to see her daughter against her.

The wife also learned that the husband had been bad-mouthing her to the child. He would tell the child she was a terrible parent and that he was going to get custody of her, so she needed to get used to how things were.

Moral of the Story

Clients sometimes ask me whether they should talk with their soon-to-be ex-spouse before they file for divorce. In an ideal world, I believe this makes sense. In some of the smoothest divorces I have handled, this has happened. However, those cases are the exception to the rule.

I believe a much more prudent course is to file first, get the spouse served, and then try and have a conversation. Had the wife in the above scenario done this, she would have had the protection of a standing order that has a section regarding not disrupting the children by:

- Changing the residence of the child
- Pulling the child out of school or daycare
- Hiding the child
- Making disparaging remarks regarding the other parent
- Discussing the litigation with the child

The standing order also covers property as to:

- Destroying, removing, concealing, encumbering, transferring, or otherwise harming or reducing the value of the estate of one or both parties.

Example #2—Stripping the House Including Taking the Pets

An unpleasant realization that families facing a divorce, are forced to accept is that their sweet little dog, cat, or other pet is not the member of the family that we sometimes believe they are. Despite the emotional attachments we have with our animals, the fact remains that they are in fact property owned by the family.

So, on your inventory list, your pet falls under the same general category as your bank accounts, lawn mower, and silverware. If this sounds harsh, it is not intended to be, but I do want to make a point of sorts.

In a recent divorce we handled, one of the most critical issues for the wife was her two dogs. Before either party hired a lawyer, the couple split up and separated. When the husband left their apartment, he took the wife's two dogs with him, along with the wife's passport, social security card, and some of her other personal items.

The wife tried to arrange an exchange on her own in a parking lot. She had some items of the husband's that were important to him. She thought he might be willing to give her back her dogs in exchange for his laptop. Unfortunately for her, he was not.

Moral of the Story

As with the previous example, if the wife had planned or gotten the assistance from an attorney early on, she might have saved herself a lot of aggravation. In her case, the same standing order that could have helped in the first example also covers pets.

The standing order says that "All parties are to refrain from harming, threating, interfering with the case, custody or control of a pet or companion animal that is possessed by a person protected by this order or a member of the family or household of a person protected by this order."

A divorce court generally will be willing to deal with pet issues. Pets in Texas are considered marital property, and a court may award pet custody in a divorce. However, if you care for your pet, it's a good idea to protect your animal ahead of time by talking to a divorce lawyer before there is a problem.

Example #3 Not Taking Everything You Care About with You

In most circumstances, it is not recommended that you leave the marital home for a variety of reasons including:
- Limited access to your children if they remain behind
- Limited access to financial records
- Limited control over what happens to personal property left behind

One of my biggest recommendations is if you do leave the house, take everything you care about with you or move it to a safe location. This is not done to be sneaky but to protect those items that are important to you. Create a list of these items that we will disclose to the other side when the time comes.

In one case where we represented a husband, he had moved out of the home but did not take some items that he cared about with him. At the time, there was no order in place saying he could not be in the marital home or take certain items out of the house. I suggested that he get these personal items.

However, he was afraid of what his wife would do if he showed up. I suggested that he do it at a time he knew she would not be the home. He again declined for various reasons.

Unfortunately for him, it would take six months before he could get back in the home. When he did, several of the items he wanted were missing including his guns. It took another six months for him to get his guns back. When they were finally returned to him, the wife had gotten her dad to disassemble the guns and they were all mixed up and in pieces.

Moral of the Story

Yes, the wife's behavior can be used against her in court. However, with a proactive action on the husband's part, he could have protected his personal property and saved himself a lot of aggravation.

Example #4 Not Securing or Safeguarding Valuable Property

One of my most memorable examples of the importance of safeguarding valuable property, comes from a consult I did with an older gentleman. Before he left the consult, he asked me for some suggestions and tips. I brought up how important it was to protect things in his home that were important to him and to move them to a safe location.

Later that week, the gentleman came back. He told me that everything I told him had come to pass and how he should have followed my advice. He said he had left the consult thinking I was paranoid, and his wife would never do any of the things I said. However, over the next few days, his wife had emptied their bank account and removed everything valuable from the house. She had also changed the lock on the safe.

The man had called a locksmith to help him get into the safe because there was about $100,000 worth of gold and cash in the safe. When the locksmith got there, it was the same locksmith his wife had called to change the combination. When they got into the safe, there was nothing inside.

Documenting Everything in the Home

I have discussed previously if you do not remove or cannot remove the items to a safe location; you can at least:

- Inventory your valuables and create a list.
- Photograph the property and date the photographs.
- Locate any proof you may have of what was given to you, inherited, or owned before the marriage.

At least in this way, you have documented the condition of the property and you can prevent your spouse from saying that the item had never existed. In another case I have handled, we have helped our clients with doing all the above.

At some point in the case, it is customary to exchange inventories and proposed property division when trying to settle a case. So, what we did for our client, in order to speed up the process of doing an inventory, was to have a couple of our paralegals show up with him at the home and photograph all the rooms and helped him create an inventory of everything in the house.

In cases where clients have taken us up on taking these preventive measures, we have so far not experienced any of the problems regarding house stripping, missing personal property, or missing valuables.

CHAPTER 16

CONFLICTING OUT ATTORNEYS

Fans of the "The Sopranos" or other TV shows regarding legal issues may already be familiar with how *conflicting out* an attorney can take place. In one episode of The Sopranos, a neighbor of Tony's, who happened to be a lawyer, suggested he make appointments with all the top divorce lawyers in North Jersey so Carmela his wife would not be able to find legal representation. Later in that episode, the audience learns that this dirty trick has worked when a lawyer tells Carmela that she cannot hire him because all the divorce lawyers she tries to meet with are conflicted out.

The Sopranos is a TV show that is set in New Jersey, but this chapter will examine how such a scenario would play out in Texas and what steps a spouse can take to prevent this dirty trick.

Can Spouses Use the Same Divorce Lawyer in Texas?

So far in my career, I have only run into one incident that I am aware of where a spouse may have been trying to deliberately try to conflict me out from representing his spouse. I will discuss that later in this chapter.

What I have run into more frequently is where a spouse will ask about whether I can represent them and their soon-to-be ex. What I let the potential clients know is that it is unethical and against the rules of Texas Professional Conduct for an attorney to represent both spouses in a divorce, as it would be considered a conflict of interest. What may be good for one spouse is not necessarily good for the other spouse.

Conflicted Out

The Texas rules regarding a single attorney representing a spouse is found in Texas Disciplinary Rules of Professional Conduct and reads as follows:

- Rule 1.05 Confidentiality of Information
- Rule 1.06(b) Conflict of Interest: General Rule
- Rule 1.09 Conflict of Interest: Former Client

Rule 1.05 states:

(a) "Confidential information" includes both "privileged information" and "unprivileged information." "Privileged information" refers to the information of a client protected by the lawyer-client privilege of Rule 503 of the Texas Rules of Evidence or Rule 503 of the Texas Rules of Criminal Evidence or by the principles of attorney-client privilege governed by Rule 501 of the Federal Rules of Evidence for United States Courts and Magistrates. "Unprivileged client information" means all information relating to a client or furnished by the client, other than privileged information, acquired by the lawyer during the course of or by reason of the representation of the client.

Rule 1.06(b)

Rule 1.06(b) tells Texas lawyers that they are to forego the dual representation in the following situations:

- Where the representation of one client is "directly adverse" to the representation of another client if the lawyer's independent judgment on behalf of a client or the lawyer's ability or willingness to consider, recommend or carry out a course of action will be or is reasonably likely to be adversely affected by the lawyer's representation of, or responsibilities to, the other client.
- The dual representation also is directly adverse if the lawyer reasonably appears to be called upon to espouse adverse positions in the same matter or a related matter.

Rule 1.09 says:

a) Without prior consent, a lawyer who personally has formerly represented a client in a matter shall not thereafter represent another person in a matter adverse to the former client:

(1) in which such other person questions the validity of the lawyer's services or work product for the former client;

(2) if the representation in reasonable probability will involve a violation of Rule 1.05; or

(3) if it is the same or a substantially related matter.

This rule has been construed by some courts to include protect potential clients who consult with attorneys regarding representation. This means that a Texas divorce lawyer may be conflicted out representing a wife if her husband consults with them even if they are not hired by the husband just like in The Sopranos.

Ethics Opinions 294 & 494

One ethics opinion I researched regarding the situation examined those rules in relation to divorce consult and came down on the side of if an attorney meets with a spouse, they cannot then represent the other spouse.

In a similar opinion, (Opinion 294, *TBJ*, September 1964) the committee found that an attorney who represented the wife in a prior divorce action, which was dismissed upon reconciliation, could not ethically represent her husband in a subsequent divorce suit filed against her by her husband. The committee reasoned that an attorney's duty to preserve a client's confidence outlasts his or her employment, and employment which involves the disclosure or use of these confidences to the disadvantage of the client.

Procedure

A party who seeks to disqualify opposing counsel must file a motion to disqualify. The person bringing this motion to disqualify an opposing counsel bears the burden of proving that disqualification is proper.

Your spouse will need more than:

- mere allegations of unethical conduct or

- evidence showing a remote possibility of a violation of the disciplinary rules to disqualify an opposing counsel.

To disqualify opposing counsel on the basis of prior representation, a party must prove three elements:

- Opposing counsel previously had an attorney-client relationship with the party;
- The pending litigation is the same as or is substantially similar to the prior representation; and
- The facts in the pending litigation create a genuine threat that the opposing counsel will reveal confidences.

Waiving the Conflict
One way to waive the conflict is if a party does not file a motion to disqualify opposing counsel in a timely manner, then they have waived the complaint. The untimely urging of a disqualification motion lends support to any suspicion that the motion is being used as a tactical weapon.

Alternatively, parties can also choose to waive the conflict of interest of an attorney having met with both parties.

Is this a Good Strategy to Utilize During a Texas Divorce?
In my opinion, I do not think it is a good approach for people to take. Taking this approach is likely to escalate the conflict between spouses and make for a more expensive divorce. Generally, I believe it is better for both spouses to have excellent divorce lawyers. This facilitates reaching a prompt and fair settlement.

When you eliminate the good divorce lawyers from the equation, this means the divorce case is likely going to take longer and be more expensive. This has been my experience both when a spouse is trying to represent himself and when an attorney who does not normally practice divorce law accepts a case. In both scenarios, someone is trying to learn divorce law and does not know what is reasonable or what a divorce court would likely do.

Although this dirty trick may be tempting, I would advise a spouse to refrain. This is more likely to have some success in towns with fewer attorneys. However, it may still have some degree of success in the city as well.

How can you prevent this from happening to you?

One way to prevent yourself from falling victim to this tactic is to meet with a divorce lawyer at the first sign a divorce may be on the table. In most circumstances, that means the Texas divorce lawyer will be unable to meet with your ex and you will have, in effect, at least one option as far as securing the services of a lawyer for your divorce.

If you are concerned about whether your spouse might do this, it would be a good idea to talk with a divorce lawyer as soon as you can. You may not be sure that you want a divorce or that you are going to get divorced. However, a divorce lawyer can discuss your options with you, make you aware of your rights, and give you some more information regarding the process. We have met with many potential clients who were feeling greatly distressed and afterward they said, "I am so glad I met with you; I feel so much better."

CHAPTER 17

QUITTING JOB TO AVOID PAYING CHILD SUPPORT

U nfortunately, some spouses do not feel an obligation to support their children after a divorce. I have heard all kinds of excuses from "I should not have to pay because I have a car note" to "I am already behind on my child support on another child."

These deadbeat parents often come up with creative plans to avoid child support. I sometimes hear them threaten that if you try and get child support then "I am going to go for full custody" or "I am going to fight for 50/50 custody, so I don't have to pay child support." All the above ideas are flawed strategies considering how Texas family law works.

I am going to discuss a strategy that is sometimes employed—quitting a job or changing your job to reduce child support obligations. This can be an effective dirty trick during a divorce or child support case, a trick a Texas divorce lawyer can help you avoid.

A Low-Paying Job or No Job Does Not Automatically Mean Less Child Support

The premise behind a parent intentionally under-employing themselves or quitting their job is because Texas calculates child support based on income; if they are making less, they will pay less in child support. After child support is set, then they can get a better job making more money.

I believe in most cases parents do not lose their jobs on purpose. However, I have had cases where a parent consciously chose to intentionally be unemployed because they were likely to be ordered to pay child support.

Quitting a job can be an incredibly bad move by a paying parent if there is a child support order in place. A parent's child support obligation continues, however long, an order is in place, requiring the parent to pay child support. A parent may seek to modify a child support order based upon the loss of a job, and the court may order the cessation of child support retroactive to the date the petition seeking to modify child support was filed by the obligor.

However, a child support modification is not something that happens automatically. The attorney general can be incredibly slow to move on a case like this. I have had potential clients meet with me who had been trying to get the attorney general to do something for five years. A family law attorney is a quicker option, but once you have quit your job, they are more difficult to pay.

Intentional Underemployment
In most cases, a Texas family law court will use a parent's actual income to calculate child support. However, the Texas Family Code 154.066 covers Intentional Unemployment or Underemployment.

(a) If the actual income of the obligor is significantly less than what the obligor could earn because of intentional unemployment or underemployment, the court may apply the support guidelines to the earning potential of the obligor.

Iliff v. Iliff, No. 09-753 (Tex. April 15, 2011)
Before this case, there was a split among the courts of appeal on how much proof was required before applying 154.066.

In this case, the Texas Supreme Court looked at the language of the statute, which states if the actual income of the obligor is significantly less than what the obligor could earn because of intentional unemployment or underemployment, the court may apply the support guidelines to the earning potential of the obligor.

The Texas Supreme Court Determined that:

- The language of Texas Family Code section 154.066 does not require such proof
- That intent to avoid child support need not be proven for the trial court to apply the child support guidelines for earning potential instead of actual earnings
- However, a trial court may properly consider an obligor's intent to avoid child support as a factor, along with other

relevant facts, in intentional unemployment or underemployment analysis

The Texas Supreme Court's interpretation of the statute allows a determining court the option to respond if a parent tries to employ a dirty trick to lower their child support. The Supreme Court reminded the courts to keep "the best interest of the child" in mind when making its determination.

If you believe your ex is trying to manipulate their income intentionally, be sure to contact an attorney.

CHAPTER 18

DIRTY DIVORCE TRICK— TURNING INTO A TEMPORARY "HELICOPTER" PARENT

Recently, we had a case where I was able to observe a husband become a "helicopter" parent. He used his new-found involvement with the children to strongly negotiate for additional time with the children and reduced child support. At the time, those involved with the case did not suspect that this behavior of his was a trick.

However, after the divorce, his behavior led the mother to believe he had just been putting on a show and had negotiated in bad faith. In this chapter, we will discuss what happened so that our readers can learn by example in case they are faced with a similar scenario.

The Suddenly Newly-Involved Parent

The wife in our story filed for divorce and then observed her once arguably absentee father become very involved with the children.

Before she filed, he did not attend the children's events such as sports or other school activities; however, he was now very involved. He was also now volunteering to take the kids to school, helping to prepare meals for the children, and taking them to their doctors' appointments.

It seemed like a miracle that now after the wife filed for divorce, her husband had turned into a very hands-on parent.

A Dream Come True

In our case, the wife was excited; she thought it was great that her husband was now showing an interest in the children. She was not suspicious and did not think he was playing games or trying to trick her. In this case, the husband and wife came up with their visitation schedule. It involved 50/50 time with the children.

In their order, the husband was still going to pay the wife child support and the wife was still going to be the "primary parent." However, because of the more equalized time, the husband was going to pay below guideline child support.

However, after the divorce, she became convinced he never had any intention of exercising his hard-fought time with the children. Instead, she now believes he only maximized his time with the children to argue for below-guideline child support.

What convinced her was that soon after the divorce, the husband took a new job in a new state and moved away. There was no way he was going to be able to exercise 50/50 time. This meant that she was going to be doing practically everything for the children without his help. To top it off, she was also going to be receiving less than guideline child support.

How to Prevent This Trick from Happening to You

Knowing if someone is attempting to pull this trick can be difficult. I have observed situations when a parent truly does want to spend more time with the children.

Our office has also seen people that were inspired to either work on their marriage or their family once they realized that things had suddenly become very real. So, the fact that a parent may be inspired to make changes and strive to be a better parent is not unrealistic.

However, it is also common for one parent to try and become very involved to try and avoid or minimize child support. In this case, the wife needed to talk to her lawyer to develop a plan on how to handle the husband's actions.

What I like to tell my clients is that I like for them to be in control of the situation.

For example, there is no reason the order could not have involved standard visitation and guideline child support. If the parents wanted to deviate from that visitation schedule, they still could have even though there is an order, if they can, both, agree. It is only when parents disagree that the order matters.

The same goes for guideline child support. If the wife decides to give him back some of his child support obligations, that is her right.

What Happened in the Case Scenario

Ultimately, the mother decided to file a motion for a new trial based on her husband's deception. The judge ruled against the mother. He was not very sympathetic as she had been represented by an attorney and had agreed to the order.

That is not to say the mother did not have a remedy; she was just going to have to do it through a new case and not through a divorce. She would need to file to modify the order based on a substantial change in circumstance.

CHAPTER 19

ENGAGING IN SPOUSAL STARVING TACTICS

What is Spousal Starving?

I often caution my divorce consults to prepare for a frequently employed dirty trick used by vindictive and controlling exes, "spousal starving." This tactic can be used by wealthy couples or couples with modest incomes. "Spousal Starving" refers to when one spouse cuts off financial access to the other spouse.

This can include:

- Emptying the joint bank account
- Removing the other spouse from a joint credit card, or
- Refusing to pay bills or buy groceries, knowing the other spouse has no access to cash
- Canceling vital services or utilities

A spouse can use this to put their ex at a disadvantage during a divorce. The goal is to get the other spouse in a financial position where they, out desperation, will accept an unfair settle-ment. This is more likely to happen if the starved spouse has no source of income or a family member who can help them. When I encounter spouses in this type of relationship, they want to know how they will pay for:

- Bills
- Food
- Take care of their children
- Pay for their attorney

The other awful part of spousal starving is that while you have no or little access to financial resources, often your ex-has plenty of funds to retain a Texas divorce lawyer at their disposal.

What Can I do if My Ex is Engaging in Spousal Starving?

Unfortunately, once spousal starving has begun, in the short term there is not a lot that can be done. I often feel for these individuals and let them know that their spouse's tactics will not be looked upon favorably once we are in front of a judge. Once you are in front of a judge, it will be possible to request spousal support and child support. However, getting there takes money and time. This future help is often hard for someone to appreciate when they are worried about getting through today.

One of the best solutions is if you can borrow money from:

- Parents or other family members; alternatively
- You may be able to take out loans or start charging things on a credit card

What Proactive Steps Can I take Now Before a Divorce?

The things I encourage clients and potential clients to do include:

- Having a separate account which your spouse cannot empty
- If you believe divorce is coming, put half of any joint account money into that separate bank account.
- Have or open credit cards that your spouse does not have access to.
- If you cannot afford a Texas divorce lawyer and you have children, you can get help through the attorney general to get child support going. Unfortunately, this process can take a long time and ultimately when you get a divorce, it may cost more because of the prior order.
- Have copies ready of all financial paperwork. This will help your attorney to get you support once you are in front of a judge.
- Make a list of all known assets, liabilities, bank accounts, real estate, business interest, and retirement accounts.
- Monitor your credit regularly.
- Get a secure mailing address which your spouse does not have access to
- Change passwords immediately to all your accounts (do not leave your spouse without access to funds).

CHAPTER 20

SHOULD I HIDE MONEY FROM MY SPOUSE TO GET READY FOR MY TEXAS DIVORCE?

Many of the people I meet with ask about how they can pay for a divorce and whether they can put money aside for a divorce fund. There are many reasons why you may want to hide money away, not necessarily for divorce, even if you are in a happy marriage. For some, having a stash of cash:

- Gives you peace of mind that you have a cushion in case of an emergency. Maybe for a divorce, maybe for some other reason like a tree falls on the roof.
- Maybe you want a fund so that you can purchase a gift to surprise your spouse for their birthday.

My mother was married to my father for over 40 years before he passed away and she had a "secret fund." It was a fund where she set aside some amount of her paycheck and deposited into her own special account "just in case."

The just-in-case could be anything from upgrading the house to paying some bill off, or money to live on because my dad was in-between jobs.

The "secret fund" was not super-secret; my dad would occasionally complain that my mom had her "secret fund" and all his paycheck was going into their joint account.

Although now that I am looking back, my dad did the same thing by putting some of his paycheck towards a 401k and my mom would occasionally complain about that.

I have read more than one article encouraging every woman to have a "just in case fund."

The articles I read were more focused on women who were married and dependent on their husbands as "breadwinners." However, does this advice still hold in today's world where more women are working and not as dependent on their husbands?

Generally, I recommend keeping a "secret cash fund" to the people with whom I consult. I believe it is appropriate and even necessary for many of the people I meet.

Sometimes my clients, or potential clients, express concerns that it may cause more problems than it is worth with their spouses. These people are often not sure if their marriage is over. I recommend you consider the consequences before you start hiding away any money.

Another thing you can consider is how you frame what you are doing with your spouse. In my example above both my mother and father had a separate quasi-secret account. My mom did not call it her divorce stash.

It was her "just in case" fund. Many finance books when they are teaching their readers how to save money encourage opening just such a bank account and having a small percentage of each paycheck put away for "just in case" which is hopefully their retirement.

Take an Active Role in the Finances

Before we get into why you may want to consider hiding away money, one thing you should do to protect yourself immediately is to learn and participate in your families' finances. Often in families, there is a division of labor where one spouse oversees all the "money-related decisions" such as:

- Balancing the checkbook,
- Paying bills, and
- Investing money

Quite frequently, we represent a spouse who has no idea about any of the finances. This generally means we are going to have to do a lot of discovery to figure out the finances for their marriage. Something you can do to help yourself if you are a spouse who is not actively involved in the finances would be to start learning about them now and to get more involved.

If you share a joint account with your spouse, you should:

- Be aware of how it is being used
- Make sure you have access to statements either online or paper
- Try and find out what other accounts are out there such as:
  » Bank accounts
  » Investment accounts
  » Retirement accounts

You should learn how much your spouse earns including:

- Commissions
- Bonuses
- Tips
- Stock options
- Other perks

These steps will help you have a better idea of whether you are getting your fair share if you end up having to divide assets due to a divorce. If you do not take steps to protect yourself, you can find that:

- You are at a disadvantage during a divorce and
- Your divorce is more expensive because of the research your lawyer must do for you to find out about your marital finances

Can I get Alimony?

If you are the spouse who does not have any income, then there is a good chance a judge may give you some temporary spousal support during the divorce. Often, I am asked, "if I can get support from my spouse, why do I need a separate account?"

The biggest reason is the divorce process can be slow and take time. I may meet with someone 3 to 9 months before they "pull the trigger" or their spouses "pulls the trigger" on a divorce. Many times, when I am meeting with them again, they feel their situation is an emergency and that we should go into court on an emergency hearing to get them immediate relief.

Unfortunately, what a court considers an emergency is not necessarily that your spouse cleaned out the bank account. You should be prepared that it may take 45-60 days to get in front of a judge for a hearing.

Keeping all this in mind, while you may be entitled to alimony from your spouse, you will still need money to live on until support is put in place.

Keep Financial Records

There is nothing legally wrong with having a "secret account" while you are married. Married couples are not legally required to have joint accounts or to disclose any existing accounts to their spouse.

However, that changes during a divorce in Texas. It is a good idea to make sure you have copies of bank statements, so if those are requested during a divorce, you will be able to provide them for your account.

For example, if your relative gave or loaned you money that you put in the account, you would then be able to show where the money came from. If the money in the account was earned during the marriage, then Texas community property rules will still apply, and it will be community property. However, if the money was a gift or inheritance, you will want to be able to document it to show that it is separate property.

What should you do?

After reading this book, you will see that my general recommendation is that you have such an account to protect yourself. However, you will need to make that decision for yourself on what is necessary to protect you and your children.

There are some advantages to having such an account including:

- It is secret
- You can control what you do with it, and
- You will have a safety net for emergencies

Some cons could include:

- Being discovered by your spouse
- Some people feel like they are sneaky etc.

You will have to decide if it is a good idea for your situation. However, if you could be placed in a situation where you have no income by your spouse, it is in your best interest to establish protection against such an event.

Your safety net could be a:

- Bank Account
- Credit Card or
- Some other financial contingency

CHAPTER 21

USING CHILDREN AS WEAPONS

One of the saddest things I have observed during divorce proceedings is when parents start to use their children as weapons. This can take several different forms:

- Withholding the children altogether from the other parent
- Making visitation contingent on paying support or some other factor
- Running away with the children to another city or state
- Engaging in parental alienation
- Crying wolf regarding family violence
- Coaching the children to lie

In this chapter, we will discuss some of these dirty tricks as well as the steps that can be taken should your ex-spouse start to do some of these things.

Withholding your Children

Unfortunately, during Texas divorce proceedings, parents can let their feelings toward their ex-spouse cloud their judgment.

Sometimes these feelings cause them to play games to punish their ex out of anger or fear. The thing I observe most frequently is parents withholding the children from the other parent and failing to consider what is in the best interest of their children.

The excuse I hear for this is generally that they do not want to let the other parent have the children because they are afraid that the other parent will not give them back. They engage in the very same activity they fear from the other parent.

You React to Spousal Starving

Maybe you decide to react to your spouse's bad behavior of cleaning out the joint bank account and leaving you broke. As a result, you decide to get back at them by not allowing them time with the children.

First, if a court order that addresses custody and visitation rights is in place and a spouse does not comply with the order, he or she can be held in contempt and even end up in jail.

Withholding children by either parent is not a good idea:

- The court does not like it when parents withhold children from each other.
- It violates standing orders in counties that have them.
- If there is an existing temporary order, this would be a violation of that order.

When there is no order or agreement in place, things become more complicated. This is usually the problem at the beginning of cases. If a parent engages in using the children as pawns before an order is put in place, a judge will take that into account, and there very well may be consequences.

Extreme Circumstances

Withholding children should be avoided unless there are extreme circumstances. These circumstances could include family violence or other concerns regarding a parent who could be endangering the children.

Other activities may rise to the level where withholding the children may be permissible. It would be a good idea to discuss any concerns with a Texas divorce lawyer.

Visitation Contingent on Paying Support

In many people's minds, time with children is somehow contingent on the payment of child support. Before a court order, there is nothing telling parents what they can and cannot do.

As we discussed above, courts do not like when parents decide to withhold the children from the other parent. Lack of support is not a good excuse. Withholding children may well get a parent in trouble. Lack of support is something a court will look at once the parties are in front of the judge for a hearing. However, a judge will not accept that as an excuse for withholding the children.

Once there are orders in place, the lack of connection between support and visitation becomes much clearer.

Texas Family Code Section 105.006 requests every Parenting Order to include the following language in capitalized bold type:

FAILURE OF A PARTY TO PAY CHILD SUPPORT DOES NOT JUSTIFY DENYING THAT PARTY COURT-ORDERED POSSESSION OF OR ACCESS TO A CHILD. REFUSAL BY A PARTY TO ALLOW POSSESSION OF OR ACCESS TO A CHILD DOES NOT JUSTIFY FAILURE TO PAY COURT-ORDERED CHILD SUPPORT TO THAT PARTY.

Judges are not even permitted to order support but disallow any physical access to the child when they deem it to be in the "best interest of the child." This usually happens in severe cases such as abuse or some sort of child endangerment.

Running Away with the Children

This is one of the more frustrating situations that can have significant legal consequences if ignored. There are two different scenarios that our office encounters regarding parents who abscond with the children:

- Before divorce paperwork is filed and
- After divorce paperwork is filed.

Before Paperwork Filed with the Court

Before divorce, unless there are court orders regarding the children, parents are free to do what they want with the children, including run away with them. This causes a lot of problems for the parent whose children were just taken away.

Usually, the parents are extremely upset when we meet with them and want to know what they can do about it. We explain the next step involves filing paperwork and getting some orders in place, letting them know what their rights are, and when it is their time to have the children.

If the parent does not ignore the bad behavior of the ex and files in time, we can usually force that parent to move back to the area. However, if they waited too long, they may have to fight the custody battle where their ex-spouse relocated, and this could require traveling to a new state or country.

After Paperwork is Filed with the Court

If you are in the middle of a divorce or a child custody dispute, it is a very bad idea to run away with the children because:

If there are court orders, you may no longer have the right to relocate with the child.

If you ignore a pending case, the other parent may be able to get orders appointing themselves as the primary parent. These orders may also severely limit your access to the child.

Engaging in Parental Alienation

Another tactic some unscrupulous parents will engage in during a divorce is intentionally trying to alienate the children from the other spouse to hurt the other spouse or to decrease the time the other parent has with the children.

Parental alienation can take many different forms including:

- Preventing the child's contact between the other parent or preventing the ex from seeing the children for more than a couple of hours a week and supervised.

- Intercepting phone calls and mail from the other parent.
- Continuously and repeatedly talking badly to the children about the other parent.
- Creating fear in the child regarding the other parent.
- Acting hurt or betrayed when the child wants to see the other parent or shows affection for the other parent.

These can be serious cases when parental alienation is involved. Generally, one of the first maneuvers that needs to be made is to get experts involved such as:

- Psychologists who are trained in spotting and dealing with alienation
- Amicus attorney to represent the child

Crying Wolf

Sadly, domestic violence can be an all too real thing for many people going through a divorce in Texas. In many cases, domestic violence is the reason for the separation and divorce proceedings. In other cases, the violence starts as a result of the divorce proceedings.

Texas Takes Domestic Violence Seriously

Texas takes domestic violence issues very seriously, and our laws allow victims to seek relief from a judge very quickly. A victim of domestic violence can be granted relief by:

- Being awarded possession of the marital home.
- Obtaining a protective order against the aggressor.
- The aggressor not being allowed within so many feet of the marital home or the victim's place of employment.

- The aggressor losing the right to possess a firearm.
- Temporary custody of the children.
- The aggressor losing the presumption that joint custody of the children is in their best interest.

Texas Domestic Violence Law as a Weapon

Unfortunately, the same law that is used to protect victims can be used as a weapon against an innocent party. This perhaps can be one of most serious and potentially damaging tactics in a divorce case.

A victim in Texas of domestic violence can:

- Have an ex-parte meeting with a judge (without the other spouse present), and if the judge believes the victim's story, the victim can be granted emergency custody of the children.
- Later there will be a hearing in court within ten days of the ex-parte order where evidence can be presented.
- However, the ex parte emergency custody order stays in place until that hearing.

Our office has not seen this manipulation of the Texas domestic violence laws often; however, it is a dirty trick you should be aware of.

It is something I bring up and caution clients about. Generally, I tell them if there is any question in their mind that their ex might make something up about them to:

- Remove themselves from the situation and do not be alone with their ex without witnesses.
- Record their interactions with their ex.

One of the few things worse than going through a divorce proceeding is to be going through a divorce proceeding and having to defend against criminal charges.

File a False Accusation of Child Abuse

I suspect that few people knowingly file false reports of abuse, but it is very prevalent for people caught in the heat of the moment of divorce to stretch normal occurrences to suit their benefit.

Be very careful when pointing fingers. If child abuse has occurred and can be proven, this can be a sword that can help your case. However, if you do not have a good reason for making accusations, this sword can be used against you very effectively to limit your access to your children.

Coaching the Children to Lie

Another tactic that parents use sometimes, is to try to coach their children to lie. This has come up in a few of my cases, and when discovered, it goes badly for the parent who is discovered. A couple of the ways I have observed parents being caught are when:

- There is an amicus involved or
- A judge has been asked to interview the child

In the case with the amicus, the amicus caught the mother coaching the children and placing recording devices on the children. The amicus, in that case, recommended the father not only be the primary parent for the children but also have sole managing conservatorship.

In the case with the judge, one of the first questions the judge asked the children is what have your parents told you to tell me.

Divorce can be extremely hard on the children. They often do not understand the reasons for the divorce, feel caught in the middle, and many times wish the parents would get back together. When parents are focused on "winning," they often lose sight of what is in the best interest of the children.

Unfortunately, coaching or prepping children is not a rare occurrence. The good news is that it is frequently discovered as in the above examples. If a child's testimony seems rehearsed and the children appear coached, generally very little weight will be placed on their testimony.

CHAPTER 22

"OH, BY THE WAY, KID #2 ISN'T YOURS."

You would think the issue of secret nonmarital children occurs only rarely, but sadly that is not the case. At the time of divorce, the father learns for the first time that one or more of the children he thought were his, were, instead, sired by his best friend, neighbor, co-worker, or some guy he has never heard of from the local pub.

Sometimes this can cause problems obtaining custody because if the biological father somehow obtains a paternity order, a major legal obstacle is created.

Now the husband and father must either try to obtain custody of only his own biological children which can be more difficult because case law and many courts have a policy against splitting up siblings, or he must try to get custody of all of the children, including those that are not his own, which can be difficult as well when you are not the biological father.

In the past 12 months, my office has represented three different husbands who were going through a Texas divorce and found themselves in a situation in which the wife had a child with another man. In some of the cases, the husband was aware that the wife had cheated on him, but not that the child was not biologically his.

The one thing that was consistent in all three of the cases was that the husband had bonded with and loved the child and did not care if the child was his biologically. They wanted to remain the father of the child with all the duties and responsibilities that this entailed even after the marriage was over.

The facts and the people were different in each one of the three cases, so all the twists and turns of the cases played out a little differently. In this chapter, I am going to discuss the various applicable Texas Laws that should be considered when contemplating a case involving paternity by Estoppel.

What is Paternity by Estoppel?

The doctrine of paternity by estoppel is most often applied in child support cases to either preclude a man who has held the child out as his own from avoiding support of the child after his relationship with the child's mother has ended.

However, it can also be used to preclude a mother who held one man out as her child's father from denying him a relationship with the child as the father later.

When I handled my first one of these cases, I remembered this doctrine from law school and thought I would ask some of my colleagues for their help in getting caught up on applying it in the real world. Unfortunately, this did not work out very well. Most of the Texas family law attorneys did not know what I was talking about. However, with a lot of research, I found a few Texas cases on point that allowed me to create the necessary tools to fight these cases in court.

Custody Battles are Expensive

One of the things I caution someone who is contemplating taking on a case involving paternity by estoppel is that it may get very expensive. This is, partly, because it is a fact-intensive issue and partly because it is also a fight regarding the conservatorship of a child.

In many of my cases, I can give my clients a guestimate regarding the range of potential costs based on where their case ends up in the process. I am also able to tell them what similar cases have averaged as far as costs, but these cases where there is some sort fight over conservatorship of a child are outliers to this range and cost averages.

Presumption of Paternity—Motion to Deny Genetic Testing

In my cases discussed above, the issue of paternity came up during the divorce process because the wives decided to bring up the fact that their husbands were not the genetic father of the child. One of my first battles in one of these cases was over DNA testing.

A wife had, on her own, without agreement or court order, conducted a DNA test and was trying to have the results admitted as evidence to prove that her husband was not the genetic father of the child. In response, we filed a "Motion to Deny Genetic Testing and Objection to Admissibility of Results of Genetic Testing."

A Court Can Deny a Motion for Genetic Testing

Under the Family Code Section 160.204, "A man is presumed to be the father of a child if he is married to the mother of the child and the child is born during the marriage."

When a child has a presumed or acknowledged father, a court can deny a motion for genetic testing based on equity. *See* Tex. Fam. Code §160.608(a), (f). To deny the motion, the court must find, based on clear and convincing evidence, that (1) the mother or father engaged in conduct that estops either party from denying parentage and (2) disproving the father's relationship with the child would be inequitable. *See id.* §160.608(a), (d), (f). In determining whether testing would be inequitable, the court must consider the child's best interest. *See id.* §160.608(b), (f). To determine the child's best interest, the court must consider the following factors:

- The length of time between the date the parentage suit was filed and the date the presumed or acknowledged father was placed on notice that he may not be the genetic father. *See id.* §160.608(b)(1), (f).
- The length of time the presumed or acknowledged father assumed the role of the child's father. *See id.* §160.608(b)(2), (f).
- The facts surrounding the presumed or acknowledged father's discovery of his possible nonpaternity. *See id.* §160.608(b)(3), (f).

- The nature of the relationship between the child and the presumed or acknowledged father. *See id.* §160.608(b)(4), (f).
- The age of the child. *Id.* §160.608(b)(5).
- Any harm that may result to the child if presumed or acknowledged paternity is successfully disproved. *See id.* §160.608(b)(6), (f).
- The nature of the relationship between the child and the alleged father. *Id.* §160.608(b)(7).
- The extent to which the passage of time reduces the chances of establishing the paternity of another man and a child-support obligation in favor of the child. *Id.* §160.608(b)(8).
- Any other factors that may affect the equities arising from the disruption of the relationship between the child and the presumed or acknowledged father or the chance of other harm to the child. *Id.* §160.608(b)(9), (f).

Genetic Testing Under Texas Family Code 160.502

If a child has a presumed, acknowledged, or adjudicated father, the results of genetic testing are inadmissible to adjudicate parentage unless performed; except:

- with the consent of both the mother and the presumed, acknowledged, or adjudicated father; or
- under an order of the court under Section 160.502.

Based on Texas Family Code 160.502, we were initially able to keep out the genetic results because they had not been conducted by agreement or by court order. We then had to have a court hearing ad described above on whether the Court would order genetic testing.

Clear and Convincing Evidence

Under Texas Family Code 160.608, to prevent the court from ordering genetic testing, the following must be shown based on clear and convincing evidence:

- the mother or father engaged in conduct that estops either party from denying parentage and
- disproving the father's relationship with the child would be inequitable.

The big challenge here is "Clear and Convincing Evidence." A medium level of burden of proof which is a more rigorous standard to meet than the preponderance of the evidence standard, but a less rigorous standard to meet than proving evidence beyond a reasonable doubt which is the standard needed to convict someone of a crime.

In one of my cases, it was easy enough to prove that the mother had engaged in conduct that estops either party from denying parentage. However, the second prong was more challenging to prove.

If you lose under the Family Code 160.608, all is not lost

Even if someone loses under 160.608 of the Family Code, then they may still be able to proceed under a common law basis for paternity by estoppel. In *Hausman v. Hausman*, 199 S.W.3d 38 (2006) the court found in that case that no statutory basis for estoppel. However, there was a basis for "equitable estoppel."

Equitable estoppel may arise if five factors are satisfied:

- There was a false representation or concealment of material facts;
- Made with knowledge, actual or constructive, of those facts;
- To a party without knowledge, or the means of knowledge, of those facts;
- With the intention that it be acted upon; and
- The party to whom it was made must have relied on the misrepresentation to his prejudice.

No Heightened Burden of Proof

Unlike section 160.608 of the Family Code. The Court found in *Hausman v. Hausman,* "Nothing in section 160.608(d) requires a heightened burden to be applied when a trial court is exercising its equitable jurisdiction to determine whether a mother is estopped from denying a presumed father's paternity.

Child Aged 4

Once a child turns four, a new statute under the Family Code becomes relevant. Under Section 160.607:

- Except as otherwise provided by Subsection (b), a proceeding brought by a presumed father, the mother, or another individual to adjudicate the parentage of a child having a presumed father shall be commenced not later than the fourth anniversary of the date of the birth of the child.

- A proceeding seeking to adjudicate the parentage of a child having a presumed father may be maintained at any time if the court determines that:
  » the presumed father and the mother of the child did not live together or engage in sexual intercourse with each other during the probable time of conception; or
  » the presumed father was precluded from commencing a proceeding to adjudicate the parentage of the child before the expiration of the time prescribed by Subsection (a) because of the mistaken belief that he was the child's biological father based on misrepresentations that led him to that conclusion.

Generally, under the Texas Family Code, there is no time limitation for a suit to adjudicate parentage if the child has no presumed, alleged, or adjudicated father.

However, to adjudicate parentage of a child with a presumed father the suit must be brought within four years of the anniversary of the child's birth.

If a parent wants to overcome this four-year limitation, a presumed father must not have lived with the mother or engaged in sexual intercourse with her during the probable time of conception. The presumed father also must never have represented to others that the child was his own.

If two people live together as husband and wife, with a child born during their marriage, and meet the requirements of Texas Family Code 160.607(b) it can be very difficult to overcome.

CHAPTER 23

THE UNENFORCEABLE
VISITATION ORDER

The unenforceable visitation order combines elements of both the "amicable divorce trick" and "using the children as weapons trick." The success of this trick is largely a result of a parent not having an attorney to protect them.

When someone with whom I have a consult asks me, "Do I need an attorney?" I will often pause and think about the variations I have seen of this trick in particular. For that reason, I will often say, "I think an attorney should represent everyone. At least that way they know what they agree to is reasonable."

Today I am going to discuss a couple of the worst tricks I have seen that have made a parent's visitation order unenforceable.

Example #1: I have a Standard Visitation Order, Don't I?

One gentleman I met had gone through a divorce while he was in the military. He had tried to make sure his family would be taken care of after the divorce. When this gentleman agreed to a visitation order, he thought he was getting standard visitation.

He learned he did not have normal visitation, when, after the divorce, he tried to exercise his visitation and his ex-wife refused to let him see his kids. She told him that he only had standard visitation when she had agreed to visitation.

The language that his ex-wife's attorney had placed in the order was for a standard visitation order. However, the attorney had also slipped this language in:

"At this time, the Home Parent and Co-Parent agree that there shall be no visitation.

If at such time the Home Parent and Co-Parent agree to allow visitation, then visitation will be

conducted as agreed in advance by the Home Parent and Co-Parent."

What this amounted to was that the gentleman had no visitation unless his ex-wife agreed to him having visitation.

Normal Provision

IT IS ORDERED that the conservators shall have possession of the child at times mutually agreed to in advance by the parties, and, in the absence of agreement, it is ORDERED that the conservators shall have possession of the child under the specified terms set out in this Possession Order.

The provision above is what should have been there. What the normal provision says is that the parents can agree to whatever they want. However, if they are not able to agree, then they need to follow the order. Then the order will go into detail of how to handle visitation.

The gentleman I met with ended up having to file to modify visitation and spend several thousand dollars to fix a few sentences in his divorce decree.

Example #2: My Wife Denies Me Access to My Children. Can I File an Enforcement?

One of the benefits a visitation order is supposed to provide is that if the other parent is not following the visitation order, you can ask the court for help in enforcing the visitation order.

Recently, I met with a different man who had recently concluded his divorce case. On the first weekend that he was supposed to exercise his visitation with his child, he arrived at his ex-spouse's home at 6:00 p.m. to pick his daughter up. He knocked at the door but there was no response.

He then texted his ex-spouse's phone but did not get a response. He left disappointed, frustrated, and angry. He wondered if this was going to become a regular occurrence. Sure enough, it did. That was why he was in my office asking about his options to make sure this does not happen again.

I explained how enforcing visitation works. The judge will need evidence regarding a violation of a court order.

A "PROPER" DENIAL OF VISITATION

Correct Place / Correct Time

First and foremost, it is important to make sure you are picking your child up at the right time, date, and location.

Once you have confirmed the date, time, and location for pickup of your child, arrive at the location in advance and wait if necessary.

Knock on the door a few times and make sure that anyone in the home is aware that you are present and ready to pick up your child. Do not just sit in your car in front of the home.

If you do these things and document, you can normally ask the court to enforce your court order.

The Problem with The Man's Order

In most visitation orders, there is a section normally titled "General Terms and Conditions." In this section, there are several important things included to make a visitation order enforceable including sections stating:

- Where pick up and drop-offs are to take place
- Orders telling the parent to release the child to the other parent
- Orders telling the parent to return the child to the other parent

This man's visitation order did not include this section of the visitation order. His order clearly stated he was entitled to visit the child. However, nothing was stating where the exchange was supposed to take place or that his ex-spouse had to turn over the child to him.

What this meant is that he did not have a remedy for enforcing the order. His only solution was to ask the court to modify the order to add *The General Terms and Conditions* section to the visitation orders, so it would be enforceable.

Example #3: Father Will Not Return the Children to Me and The Police Will Not Help

In a different consult, I met with a woman who informed me that she had full custody of her children. She had let the children go visit their dad in Dallas, but he was refusing to return the children to her.

She had also reached out to the police who had refused help her. They told her it was a civil matter, and she needed to hire an attorney. I reviewed her order and noticed several problems with it.

Her order did give her sole custody of all the decision-making rights. The attorney in the child support office appears to have tried to pull a similar trick as the one from the first example in this chapter.

However, the attorney left out the line "IT IS ORDERED AND DECREED that mother shall have possession of the child at all times not specifically awarded in this decree to FATHER or otherwise mutually agreed by the parties."

The attorney also left out the "General Terms and Condition Section."

What the attorney had included was a one-sentence visitation order "IT IS ORDERED that the conservators shall have possession of the child at times mutually agreed to in advance by the parties."

This meant that the lady I was meeting with did not have a visitation order saying that she had any superior right to the child or that the father had to return the child to her.

Her remedy, as in the previous scenarios, was to file to modify her order.

Combatting the Dirty Trick

The easiest way to prevent these types of problems is to be represented by an attorney whose primary practice is family law.

An attorney who has experience with 1) Divorce, 2) Child Custody, and 3) Enforcing Divorce and Child Custody Orders will be able to recognize this trick and ensure the proper language is in your final order.

CHAPTER 24

THE TRICK OF USING DELAY TACTICS

Two of the most frequently asked questions I get during my Houston divorce consults are:

- "How much is my divorce going to cost?" and
- "How long is my divorce going to take?"

It is understandable that anyone about to undergo a divorce would like to know the answers to these questions. We all would like some certainty in our lives. Unfortunately, in the Texas divorce process, there is a lot of uncertainty. In this chapter, we will discuss the dirty trick of delaying the divorce, reasons why it is sometimes used, and methods of combatting this dirty divorce trick.

What are Some Reasons a Spouse May Want to Delay the Divorce?

Some of the reasons I have observed as to why spouses want to delay a divorce include:

- To punish their ex
- Having a scorched-earth mentality
- To obtain a financial benefit

Punish Spouse

I have witnessed this happen on more than one occasion. The first time that I experienced this, was early in my legal career, and I was working as an associate for another attorney. In that case, our client was a music teacher, and from what I recall, he made approximately $40,000 a year. His ex-spouse ran up the litigation costs and turned what should have been a $5,000 divorce into a $40,000 divorce. She did this by conducting unnecessary requests for production:

- Asking for bank account documents from 10 years ago
- Depositions regarding bank accounts and other financial accounts
- Motions to compel and other needless hearings

Her excuse was that she was trying to find out if her husband the music teacher was hiding assets in offshore bank accounts. I believe the real reason was she was trying to punish her husband. That case did involve adultery. However, in the process of punishing her husband, she also managed to punish herself. They were in a large financial hole after the divorce.

Scorched Earth or Win at All Costs Mentality

This is one way I have seen tactical and stalling measures used. Another attorney I know had a consult where a husband wanted to figure out how to dispose of all the marital property so that the wife did not get anything. He would rather they both walk away with nothing, than have her walk away with anything.

Unfortunately, someone with this sort of attitude can easily and deliberately drive up the costs for the other spouse. This is sometimes done to try and financially squeeze the spouse, or wear them down, so they are too frustrated to continue the litigation.

Financially Beneficial

Another reason why your ex may want to delay the divorce is that they are receiving temporary spousal support (alimony). If they are not eligible for post-divorce spousal support, then they have a vested interest in trying to extend the pendency of a divorce case for a long period of time.

Some Methods Used to Delay the Texas Divorce Process

The Texas divorce process can be costly at the best of times. However, some vindictive divorcing spouses can manage to double, triple, or even quadruple their divorce litigation costs. Through their actions, they also intentionally inflict similar inflated costs on their future exes. This is done by:

- Avoiding service
- Changing lawyers frequently
- Failing to respond to discovery
- Not signing documents
- Not returning phone calls, emails, or other forms of communication
- Bringing needless motions
- Generally dragging out the process

Avoiding Service of Process

One of the most common delaying tactics is by avoiding service. The next step after filing for divorce is to bring your spouse under the power of the court. This is done by serving them with a copy of the divorce paperwork. However, if your ex-spouse avoids service, this will delay the divorce process.

If your spouse avoids normal service, your divorce lawyer can ask the court for substituted service. This is an order from the court allowing service in an alternative manner such as:

- Publication in a newspaper
- Posting a copy of the divorce paperwork on the door where your spouse is staying
- Serving anyone over the age of 16 at the residence where your spouse is staying
- The most common forms of substitute service granted by courts are:
- Service on any person over sixteen years of age in the house or
- Attaching the process to the front door of the confirmed residence of the spouse
- If the residence is unknown, then it is common to serve the party by publication. The downsides to substituted service are:
- Generally, this method costs more
- Takes longer
- If a judgment is reached by default, then your spouse, has the opportunity, to ask for a new trial up to two years later. This could mean more legal fees and more delays.

Firing Your Lawyer Just Before Trial

This divorce trick of firing their Texas divorce lawyer a few weeks before trial, can sometimes be used effectively to delay a divorce.

The fact that a spouse is generally free to make a change in lawyers, mid-case, does not necessarily mean it is a good idea to do so. Yes, it may delay the trial. However, the tradeoff is:

- The new attorney will be scrambling to get caught up regarding the facts of the case that may have been going on for a year or more.
- You are paying your new lawyer for the time they spend learning the facts that your old attorney will already have known.
- Your new attorney will probably require a large retainer
- If you owe your old attorney any money, they may intervene in your divorce case to collect that money. This can add additional costs to what is probably already an expensive divorce.

How does this work?

In general, a client has a right to be represented by the lawyer of their choosing. That means, in most circumstances, they can change attorneys, mid-case.

Judges are not generally inclined to force clients to stay in contractual relationships against their will. However, at times divorcing spouses can try and use their ability to fire and hire new counsel to their advantage.

At its most simple level firing your lawyer is a reason to ask for a continuance from the court to:

- Find a new lawyer
- For your new lawyer to get up to speed on the case

Unless this trick has been used more than once. A court is often inclined to grant this motion for continuance.

How to Combat Your Spouse's Delaying Tactics

Depending on the case, there are different things that can be done to combat delaying tactics. Unfortunately, most of the time the remedy is not immediate. However, it is possible to push a case along.

Not Complying with Discovery

Usually, in the divorce cases I have handled, everyone understands that they are expected to comply with the discovery rules of a case. Unfortunately, there are times when this does not happen, or the discovery is not completed promptly.

Most of the time when there is an attorney on the other side of the case, we can reach an agreement on when they will get us the needed discovery. However, there have been times when there is a non-attorney or a difficult attorney on the other side of the case.

When this happens, the remedy is to file a motion to compel discovery and set it for a hearing. If after the hearing a judge finds that your ex-spouse violates the discovery rules, a judge can:

- Disallow further discovery by the violating party
- Order the costs of discovery be paid by the violator
- Order that the violating party cannot raise defenses or claims
- Strike all or parts of the violator's pleadings
- Find the violator in contempt

Generally, a judge must start with something mild before working up to the harsher discovery remedies. However, if your ex-spouse continues to be difficult, the penalties can become very harsh.

Not Signing an Agreed Order

If the agreement was reached in mediation, then an added benefit of mediation is that we can get the court to sign an order based on that agreement. The easiest way to proceed of course is if everyone complies with signing the order, to begin with.

However, sometimes people change their minds, get cold feet, or want to tweak the agreement. In these cases, we will set a hearing to prove up the mediated settlement agreement. The judge will give our office a certain amount of time to draft and circulate an order based on that agreement.

If the other side continues to refuse to sign, we will show up on the day of entry (the date the judge gave us to come back if the order was not signed by all parties). Provided that, the Final Divorce Decree or other order that has been, drafted, is based on the mediated agreement a judge will still sign the Order even if your ex or the opposing counsel refuses.

Order Based on a Court Hearing

The above method of getting an order signed applies to any order based on a hearing in front of a judge. The only difference is there is not the added step of proving up the agreement first. That is because there is already a hearing and the order is based on the ruling by the judge.

Asking for Extensions, Missing Depositions, or Missing Mediation Dates

A divorce case can become very frustrating if your ex-spouse refuses to respond, does so slowly, or does whatever they can to drag their feet. Examples include:

- Requesting extensions
- Canceling depositions
- Being too busy to schedule a mediation or missing mediation dates

The remedy when these types of tactics start to happen is much like others we have already discussed—filing a motion and going to court. This can be very frustrating for clients because the remedy seems like "just another delay." Unfortunately, to push the case forward, it sometimes requires the help of the court. If your ex is dragging their feet regarding mediation or complying with depositions, a judge can order:

- The reimbursement by your ex of attorney's fees and any other costs associated with enforcing compliance.
- Dates when mediation and depositions must be completed
- Other sanctions if your ex-spouse fails to comply with the judge's orders

CHAPTER 25

FILING FOR DIVORCE IN ANOTHER CITY

Many of my potential clients are concerned with filing first in their divorce case. Many of them have the impression that if they are not the first to file, they will be at a disadvantage in their case. In many cases, this is generally not the case when both spouses are represented by divorce lawyers.

However, there are some exceptions to this rule. One of those is when the spouses are in different cities. In such a case filing first can provide a real strategic advantage.

In this chapter, we will focus on how choosing the battleground of where to file for divorce can impact divorce proceedings when spouses live in different counties.

Choosing Which County to File In

In most divorce cases, there is not an option on where to file a divorce. This is because Texas Family Code Section 6.301 sets out the residency requirements for filing for divorce. Those requirements are that at least one spouse must have been:

- a domiciliary of this state for the preceding six-month period; and
- a resident of the county in which the suit is filed for the preceding 90-day period.

What this section says is that if both spouses live in the same county in Texas, then there is only one option on where the spouses can file. However, if spouses live in different counties, then there is possibly a choice.

Why should I care if the divorce is in one county or another?

There are some reasons why choosing one county over another can make a difference. One of the biggest reasons is when the counties are several hours apart such as Bexar County versus Harris County. In such a case this would mean:

Convenience

One spouse would have a much more convenient forum for their divorce. While their spouse would have to make a trip that takes hours back and forth whenever there is a court hearing.

Additional costs

The distance can also create additional costs such as time off work, fuel costs, or having to rent a hotel whenever they are required to travel.

Local Attorney or Attorney in City where Case is Filed

Another decision the spouse, who must travel, will need to make is whether to hire an attorney near them, who will also have to travel, or an attorney in the county where the divorce is filed. Either choice will have pluses and minuses.

If they hire an attorney them, it will be more convenient to meet to discuss and prepare the case. However, whenever there is a hearing, they will be paying that attorney to travel which can be costly. This attorney may also not be as familiar with the local rules for the divorce court in that county.

If they hire an attorney in the county where the divorce is filed, meeting with that attorney to prepare, will be more inconvenient. However, they will not be paying that attorney as much for travel, and that attorney is more likely to be familiar with the local rules for the divorce court in that county.

The Race to the Courthouse

If both spouses are aware that the divorce is coming and that they are living in separate counties, then it may be obvious that they need to race to the courthouse, so that they can control where the divorce proceedings will take place.

The Dirty Trick in Action

One example of this trick in action is in a case where we represented the husband. His wife left him and moved to San Antonio where her parents lived and immediately filed for divorce and got him served.

The husband then contacted and hired our firm. We, then, immediately filed for divorce and got her served.

What happens when there are two divorce cases pending in Texas?

The issue is whether (or not):

- the husband is entitled to seek a divorce in one Texas county when
- the wife filed first in a different Texas county.

Dominant Jurisdiction

As a (general) rule, when the suit would be proper in more than one county, the court in which suit is first filed acquires dominant jurisdiction to the exclusion of other courts. See Wyatt v. Shaw Plumbing Co., 760 S.W.2d 245, 248 (Tex.1988).

Any subsequent suit involving the same parties and the same controversy must be dismissed if a party to that suit calls the second court's attention to the pendency of the prior suit by a plea in abatement.

Exceptions to the Rule

There are three exceptions to the rule:

- Conduct by a party that estops him from asserting prior active jurisdiction;
- Lack of persons to be joined if feasible, or the power to bring them before the court; and
- Lack of intent to prosecute the first lawsuit

See Wyatt v. Shaw Plumbing Co., 760 S.W.2d 245, 248 (Tex.1988).

Estoppel Example

In Clawson v. Millard, 934 S.W.2d 899, 901 (Tex. App. 1996), the husband asserted in the second court (Galveston) that even though the wife filed for divorce in Houston first, the Galveston court had dominant jurisdiction because exceptions to the general rule of dominant jurisdiction applied.

The husband claimed that the wife was estopped from relying on the fact that she filed first in Harris County because she waited four and one-half months to have him served with the citation in the Houston suit, and that by the time he was served, he had already filed for divorce in Galveston and had previously served the wife with a citation.

The Galveston court agreed and ruled in favor of the husband.

Combatting the Dirty Trick—Seek Legal Advice Immediately

If your spouse is threatening to move out of state or has already moved out of state, you will want to seek legal advice immediately to go over your legal rights. This is not a situation you want to take lightly.

The consequences of delay are severe. You do not want to be fighting your case in another state or two states.

CHAPTER 26

THE DIRTY TRICK OF MOVING OUT OF STATE WITH THE KIDS

I have seen spouses use the trick of moving out of the state with the children very effectively to the detriment of the other spouse during a divorce. However, in some cases, this move can backfire, and a judge will grant custody of the children to the other spouse because of what the court believes to be wrongful conduct.

We will now touch on the topic of parents moving out of state with their children and how this can impact divorce proceedings.

Is it Illegal for a Parent to Move out of State without the Permission of the Other Parent?

If it happens before there is an order of the court in place regarding custody, then no. Both parents have equal rights to possession of and access to the child.

Either parent can make decisions regarding the child without consulting with or notifying the other parent before making that decision.

The solution to this problem is to get a court order identifying what each parent's rights and duties are to the children.

Can I Keep the Other Parent from Leaving the State with my Children if there is an Order?

In most cases, no. When it is your time to have the children, it is your time. When it is the other parent's time to have the children, it is their time. This means either of you can leave the state when it is your time.

However, sometimes through negotiations, travel restrictions can be put in place. Alternatively, if there are some extenuating circumstances, a court will decide on a case-by-case basis if additional restrictions are needed.

What State Has the Right to Make Orders Regarding the Child?

Under Texas Family Code 152.201, a new case can be established regarding a child if:

- The state is the "Home State" of a child on the date the commencement of the proceeding.
- A court of another state does not have jurisdiction or has declined jurisdiction.

Under the Texas Family Code Section 152.102, Texas has defined "Home State" to mean "the state in which a child lived with a parent or a person acting as a parent for at least six consecutive months immediately before the commencement of a child custody proceeding. In the case of a child less than six months of age, the term means the state in which the child lived from birth with a parent or a person acting as a parent."

Home State and Divorce Proceedings

What the above statute means is that the only state that can make orders regarding a child is the state in which the child has lived for the last six months.

Why am I Paying Child Support for Children I do not Get to See?

As I mentioned in the introduction, moving to another state can be an effective dirty trick. One reason for this is if you wait for six months to file for divorce, Texas will lose jurisdiction over the children. This means:

- Texas cannot make visitation orders
- Texas cannot give you any decision-making rights
- Texas cannot force your ex to move back to Texas with the children

However, Texas can force you to pay child support for your children under Texas Family Code 159.401:

- A parent can ask for the establishment of child support in Texas even though the child does not reside in Texas
- Provided that, the parent on whom child support is to be established is in Texas

Can I make the Other Parent Move Back to Texas?

One of the questions I frequently get asked when a parent has moved to another state with the children is "can I make the other parent move back to Texas?"

If Texas is still the home state of the children, an approach I have seen Family Courts use is to give a parent the choice of:

- Either moving back to Texas with the children or
- Staying where they are and turning over the children to their ex

This means if you would like to ask the court for this relief, it is important that you file for divorce before your ex-lives in the new state for six months.

What if Texas is no Longer the Home State of the Children?

If Texas is no longer the Home State:

- In most circumstances, Texas cannot make any orders regarding the child other than child support.
- However, if you still want to get a divorce in Texas, you are still able to do so.

I have had cases where:

- A parent was not interested in receiving any visitation and just wanted to be divorced.
- I have also had cases in which they did want visitation but wanted to get the divorce part over with.

Seek Legal Advice Immediately

If your spouse is threatening to move out of state or has already moved out of state, you will want to seek legal advice immediately to go over your legal rights. This is not a situation you want to take lightly.

The consequences of delay are severe. You do not want to be fighting your case in another state or two states.

THE DIRTY TRICK OF GETTING MARRIED AGAIN

Being a divorce attorney has given me a front-row seat to people behaving badly, sometimes in a mercenary manner. I am not suggesting that anyone wanting to marry their ex-spouse again after a divorce has an ulterior motive or is trying to pull one over on their ex. However, depending on the facts involved in your situation, I would suggest it may be prudent to slow things down, to think twice about the remarriage, and to consult with a family law attorney first.

Another thing to consider is that the person you are about to remarry is the same person. A high school teacher of mine told me two things that stuck with me to this day. Those things are:

- "People do not change. They just become more of who they already are."
- "You cannot change the crazy behavior of other people. You can only change your crazy behavior."

193

For the most part, I have found those statements to be true. If you go into a relationship hoping someone is going to change, you are probably going to be disappointed. If you hang in there hoping their behavior which is driving you crazy is going change, you will be disappointed. What you do have control over is yourself and what you do.

Marrying an Abuser for the Second Time

Our firm helped a woman to obtain a divorce from a man who was physically abusive to her and her child. This was not the first time that she had divorced this man, and the man had not suddenly changed and become abusive.

This woman had already divorced him once before for being abusive. During her first divorce, she had received:

- Sole custody of the child
- A protective order against the man

Somehow, this man had convinced her he had changed and then persuaded her to move back in with him and to remarry him.

The Man Had Not Changed

Protective orders are good for two years. This man was smart and waited two years before filing for divorce himself. The man was able to hold things together long enough for the protective order to run out before he let himself go again and started abusing this woman physically.

CPS took the side of the wife's abuser.

The man had been planning this for a while and had called CPS on her for abuse of their child. CPS did not know their history and convinced her to sign a safety plan where her abuser would have the child.

The Wife Filed Another Protective Order and Struck Out

The wife tried to get another protective order against her husband. Unfortunately for her, the judge did not give her one. The judge did not like the fact that the wife had married her abuser a second time. The judge also did not like that the wife had a CPS case pending against her.

Divorce for the Second Time—Wife had Lost Her Position of Strength

Although the wife had won sole custody in her first case, she had to fight that battle for a second time all over again. This is because when she remarried her husband, all prior custody orders and child support orders were terminated.

Standard Language in Many Divorce Decrees—Termination of Orders

The language terminating orders regarding the child is standard in many child custody orders. It generally resembles the following:

"The provisions of this decree relating to conservatorship, possession, or access terminate on the remarriage of **HUSBAND to WIFE** unless a nonparent or agency has been appointed a conservator of the children under chapter 153 of the Texas Family Code."

This meant she was starting all over again. Had her husband not remarried her and had tried to gain custody of their child through a modification of the court order, he would have been fighting an uphill battle that he would most likely lose.

However, as a result of his remarriage to her, he was no longer coming from behind. There was not a protective order in place against him, and he did not have to deal with the prior order that gave the woman sole custody of the child.

In fact, with CPS investigating her for child abuse, he was walking into court slightly ahead. The case had many twists and turns and a happy ending.

An Ounce of Prevention is Worth a Pound of Cure
However, the woman could have avoided all the problems had she not remarried this man. Another thought is to ask your attorney about removing that standard provision in a child custody order.

CHAPTER 28

THE DIRTY TRICK OF COMMON LAW MARRIAGE

In Texas, many people are aware that Texas recognizes common-law marriage. However, not everyone I meet with is aware of what it takes to meet the Texas statutory requirements of being common law married or why it is important.

I have had some consults recently that made me think this topic should be included in any discussion regarding divorce tricks because when used, whether successfully or not, it can cause major aggravation, be very expensive, and take a lot of time defending it.

Scenario #1—You May Be Married if you Tell People you are and Act Married

Recently, I was meeting with a man who was bewildered that he had been sued for divorce. When I asked him about his case, he plopped down an original petition for divorce and said, "I want to know how I am married."

"Am I married?" Seems like a simple question, right? Sometimes, however, it is not. I asked him "Have you ever had a ceremonial marriage?" He said "No." I then started asking him the following questions:

Q: "Have, you ever lived together?"
Answer: "Yes."

Q: "Have you ever introduced each other as being husband and wife?"
Answer: "Yes, out of convenience."

Q: "Have you ever filed taxes together?"
Answer: "Well, we have kids together, so I filed as head of household and claimed her and the kids on my tax return."

I let him know that he and his ex may be common-law married. "Common-law marriage is something that exists in Texas, although it is called Informal Marriage under the Family Code."

Scenario #2—Be Careful Cohabitating After a Divorce

I generally will caution my clients about cohabitating after the divorce. This is because someone who ended up hiring us came in very confused after his wife had sued him for a divorce.

The reason for his confusion was because he already divorced her. He and his ex-wife had only been married for a few years and divorce had netted her practically nothing by way of a property settlement. This was because of their short-term marriage, the fact that they had no children, each took from the marriage whatever they brought and not much more.

Not long after the divorce, his ex-wife fell on hard times, and he felt sorry for her, so he let her move back in the home. She did not have a job or access to health insurance, so he got her added to his insurance policy by telling them they were married.

As a result, his ex-wife had the benefit of his dental coverage, hospital, medical, surgical, and all other insurance. His wife scheduled herself appointments at the dentist, ophthalmologist, and plastic surgeon.

His ex-wife ended up getting:

- Dental surgery
- Lasik surgery
- A facelift
- A tummy tucks
- Breast enhancement

This gentleman told me his ex-wife convinced him that all these things were a good idea and he would benefit from them. He also gave in partly out of guilt regarding the divorce.

He also conceded to help her buy a new wardrobe. Eventually, he did start to protest as the bills started to rack up. Whenever he did, she would fly off the handle and guilt him. While they had only been married previously for three years, they stayed together after the divorce for six years.

When his ex-wife filed for divorce again, as previously mentioned, it took my consult by surprise because he thought he had already divorced her. He never considered that Texas common-law marriage law might force him to divorce her again.

After I explained how Texas common-law marriage worked, he let me know he would not make the same mistake again.

Scenario #3—Doing a Cost-Benefit Analysis

Our law firm has represented clients both for and against a common law divorce. Some of these cases have ended up going to trial. This includes twice before a jury. In the majority of family law cases, it makes economic sense to settle a case before it ever reaches the trial stage. This is because the longer a case drags on, the more expensive a case is.

Jury trials also tend to be more expensive than trials before a judge. One big reason for this is that jury trials often take longer to try. At the very least, there is an extra day to pick the jury. However, there is often more stopping and starting when a jury is involved.

This is because some arguments take place outside of the jury's ears. This means the bailiff must escort the jury outside the room. Alternatively, the judge will call the lawyers to come back to the judge's chambers. All these things often add up to several more days of trial.

Having defended and tried cases involving the issue of a common-law marriage, I can say with experience that it makes a case quite a bit more expensive. On the low end, if a party contests the existence of a common-law marriage, it adds at least another $20,000. However, if the case has to be taken to trial, that number can easily double or triple.

For this reason, I will often do a cost-benefit analysis with my clients if they want to defend against the existence of a common-law marriage. If the "marriage" is short and there is not a lot of common law property, it may be quite a bit cheaper just to admit there is a marriage and divide up what little community property there is.

In a consult, a gentleman came to meet with me to get a second opinion. He was currently represented and had been defending against a common-law marriage. The man had already spent about $60,000 and had not made it to trial yet. I also found out it was going to a jury trial.

From my discussions with this man, I was able to pinpoint that if they were married, it had only been for about three years. This was because before that time period, he had been married to someone else. In Texas, you can only be married to one person at a time, so it was impossible to be married until after his divorce took place.

The man was concerned that if he admitted marriage, then his new "wife" would get a large portion of his assets. From questioning, it did not sound like there was much community property. The majority of his assets would be his separate property.

It also sounded like he had created a nice paper trail for a common-law marriage. He had emailed someone that the woman in question was his wife. He told me "I just did that, so she could sell/

show my house. She does not have a real estate license." The man had also listed the woman in his will as his common-law wife.

From what I was hearing, it sounded like this man was spending $1,000 for every dollar he was trying to save.

Scenario #4—A Common-Law Marriage is Just as Good as A Ceremonial Marriage

A while back, I met with a gentleman who was deeply concerned that his wife may get a portion of the fortune he could acquire after he received a patent and his invention went on the market. From talking to him, I learned his marriage was a common-law marriage.

Once I learned that he had a common-law marriage, I started to ask him questions. When I went through my usual questions, it started to sound like he might not have a common-law marriage. I then asked him why he thought he might be married. "Well, we signed an affidavit of informal marriage."

Through further discussions, the gentleman was hoping I would tell him that a common-law marriage was not as good as a ceremonial one. I let him know a common-law marriage is just as good as a ceremonial marriage.

This upset my consult. He did not like hearing that his patent may be community property. He told me, "but it's only a common-law marriage. Why would she be entitled to my patent? It is only in my name."

When he said that, I knew he did not understand what I was saying. I decided to try giving him an analogy. I told him, "If you have sex with someone and get them pregnant, are they any less pregnant than if they go to the doctor and get pregnant by in vitro fertilization?"

I explained to him common-law marriage is like that. "You are not any less married just because it is a common-law marriage."

My consult concluded that he should never have signed the affidavit of informal marriage. His wife had convinced him that it would a good idea for them sign the affidavit. However, he never felt like he had benefited from the affidavit and only she had.

What Is A Declaration of Informal Marriage in Texas?

If you and your spouse agree, the two of you can sign a 'Declaration of Informal Marriage' and file it with the county clerk.

Under Texas Family Code Section 2.401(a)(1), the county clerk serves as prima facia evidence that the parties have entered an informal marriage.

One thing a Declaration of Informal Marriage allows a couple to do is choose the date of their marriage.

Is Common-Law Marriage a Texas Thing?

In the above consult, the man was extremely frustrated that Texas had laws that recognize the common-law marriage. However, Texas is not the only state. The following states have laws regarding common-law marriage:

Alabama	Colorado	District of Columbia	Georgia (if created before 1/1/97)
Idaho (if created before 1/1/96)	Iowa	Kansas	Montana
New Hampshire (for inheritance purposes only)	Ohio (if created before 10/10/91)	Oklahoma (possibly only if created before 11/1/98.	Pennsylvania (if created before 1/1/05)
Rhode Island	South Carolina	Texas	Utah

The Texas Statutory Requirements for A Common-Law Marriage

An informal or common-law marriage is a marriage between two people who have not obtained a marriage license and participated in a marriage ceremony and under Texas Family Code Section 2.401:

- Agree to be married
- Live together in Texas as husband and wife and
- Hold themselves out to others in Texas as husband and wife

Agreement to be Married

One of the elements to establish a common-law marriage is the parties must agree to be married.

This means that in an evidentiary hearing, the spouse alleging a common-law marriage will need to put on evidence that the parties intended to have a present, immediate, and permanent marital relationship wherein they both agreed to be husband and wife.

An agreement to get married at some later time in the future is not sufficient to establish an agreement to be married. If there is no written agreement to be married, your actions and the actions of the other party can be used to prove that there was an agreement to be married.

Living Together

The next element needed to establish a common-law marriage is that the parties must have lived together in Texas as husband and wife.

Texas case law states that to meet the element of living together as husband and wife, you must demonstrate that you maintained a household and did things that are commonly done by a husband and a wife.

There is no minimum number of days you must have resided together in Texas to meet this requirement.

Holding Out

The final element needed to establish a common-law marriage is that parties must have told other people in Texas that they were married.

This can be accomplished either by:

- Spoken words or
- Actions and conduct by each person may be enough to fulfill the requirement of holding out.

In other words, there can be no secret common-law marriage.

Is There A Statute of Limitations on Establishing A Common-Law Marriage?

No. Contrary to what some people believe, there is no statute of limitations for establishing a common-law marriage. Provided that the elements are met that:

- There's an agreement to be married
- The couple tells other people about it and
- The couple could live together for even one day

This could be enough to establish a common-law marriage.

Legal Effect of a Common-Law Marriage

If a common-law marriage exists, it has the same legal significance as a ceremonial marriage. This means:

- You would have to file for divorce when the relationship ends just as you would if you had a ceremonial marriage.
- Once a common-law marriage is established, the only way to end it is by death, divorce, or annulment.
- There is no such thing as a common-law divorce.
- If a common-law marriage exists, then all property and debts accumulated during the duration of the common-law

marriage that are community property are subject to division by the court at the time of the divorce.

Alternatively, a couple can file a "declaration of informal marriage" under Texas Family Code Section 2.401(a)(1) with the county clerk as prima facia evidence that the parties have entered an informal marriage.

Practically speaking, if there are children resulting from a common-law marriage or property acquired during the term of the marriage, as a divorce is sometimes the best and easiest way to dissolve the relationship.

One example of this is from a case where I represented a mother who, in addition to having a child with the father, purchased a home with him. Unfortunately, when I looked at the elements to see if we could establish a common-law marriage, there was no evidence in support.

It was easy enough to establish orders regarding the child. Unfortunately, disentangling her from the house could not be accomplished at the same time and had to be pursued in a different lawsuit. This was frustrating for her because the father was living in the house rent-free and was not paying any of the bills.

Why You May Want to Deny the Existence of a Common-Law Marriage

The main reason people want to prove that a common-law marriage exists is stuff or property. They want to divide up property that may have been acquired during the marriage.

THE TEXAS DIVORCE HANDBOOK

That also happens to be the most common reason why someone wants to deny the existence of a common-law marriage. They want to avoid allowing their alleged spouse from getting community property rights over any of the property.

If the party with most of the property can prevent the existence of a common-law marriage being proven, then the alleged spouse has no rights to their property.

Proving Two People Are Common-Law Married

One of the biggest ways a common-law marriage is different than a ceremonial marriage is, if it is contested, the spouse alleging a marriage will need to put on proof.

If the marriage is contested, it may be necessary to have a mini-trial or evidentiary hearing on the existence of the marriage. If the jury or judge finds in favor of marriage, then the divorce process will proceed as normal.

Some evidence of a common-law marriage could include:

- Filing a federal income tax return with the other person named as your spouse;
- Obtaining a life insurance policy and identifying the other party as your spouse and designating them as beneficiary;
- Purchasing a home or other real property where the deed is signed by you and the other person as husband and wife;
- Taking out a loan with the other person being identified as either your husband/wife;
- Sending cards or letters to the other party that state "from your loving husband," or "to my loving wife;"

- Hosting or attending an event where you introduce the other person as your spouse;
- Your family members referring to a spouse as their son-in-law or daughter-in-law;
- Introducing the other person to your colleagues, neighbors, and friends as your husband/wife.

Does Texas Recognize Common-law marriages from the Other States?

Maybe. To prove the existence of a marriage that purportedly occurred in another state or foreign country, the party alleging a marriage will need to perform a foreign-marriage analysis.

This is done by answering a series of questions aimed at determining whether Texas Law or the law of the foreign state or country applies and whether under that law, the requirements for proving up a marriage have been met.

These questions include:

- Were the marriage requirements met under the law of either state?
- Which state's law controls?
- Texas Public Policy
- Full Faith & Credit Clause

Public Policy

If a Texas court refuses to recognize a foreign marriage because it violates Texas public policy, the parties to the foreign marriage can return to the state or country where the marriage took place and seek a divorce there.

Full Faith & Credit

Under the full faith and credit clause, each state must give full faith and credit to the judicial proceedings, public acts, and records of other states.

Some Texas courts have held that because marriage is not a judicial judgment and is more like a contract or a license, a marriage in one state has never been considered constitutionally entitled to automatic recognition in other states.

CHAPTER 29

NON-MARITAL CONJUGAL COHABITATION AGREEMENTS FOR THE UNMARRIED COUPLE IN TEXAS

O ver the past six months, I have met with several potential clients who decided to make some major financial deci sions with their boyfriend or girlfriend and unfortunately the relationship did not work out.

In one case, I met with a lady who had purchased a house and had a child with her boyfriend. Both were named on the deed. In that case, the boyfriend was refusing to help support the child or contribute to any bills related to the house. He was very happy letting his girlfriend support him while he sat at home playing video games. The woman I met with wanted out and wanted to get some orders regarding the child.

In another case, a woman again purchased a house with her boy-friend; however, in that case, she was not listed on the deed but had contributed a large amount of money to the house. In this case, he kicked her out of the house and told her not to come back and that she would not see a penny of the money she had paid to the purchase of the house.

In both cases, I hoped that there would be enough evidence to support a claim of common law marriage. If there was a common-law marriage, that would be the easiest way to untangle the couple from each other financially and otherwise. Unfortunately, aside from them having lived together, there was no other evidence. Both women were adamant in that they had never intended to be married and had never held out to anyone that they were married.

This was disappointing because it meant that things would be more complicated and expensive if we were going to be able to help. Her situation is one of the reasons divorce exists. However, divorce is not available to unmarried couples.

In the first scenario, we would be able to help get orders in place regarding the child. The woman was also protected because she was on the deed; however, we would have to bring a separate lawsuit regarding that property. In the second scenario, the woman might be out of luck all together; we would have to dig in deeper to see what we could do.

What rights do unmarried couples have?
Both women wanted to know if living together provided them with any sort of rights or protection. In short, the answer is no.

This is especially true concerning property acquired during a relationship. Marital property laws and other family laws were designed to protect married couples and do not apply to unmarried couples. This is true no matter how long the relationship was.

Palimony is not a legal concept. Rather, it is a popular term used to describe the division of property or periodic support payments paid to one partner in an unmarried couple by the other after the couple breaks up.

The Texas Family Code does not provide for "palimony." This means you cannot gain rights under the Texas Family Code because you lived with someone absent a valid marriage.

Can an unmarried couple establish rights as a couple?
It is possible to draft an agreement which might provide for some of the things that could be obtained with a valid marriage.

The Texas Family Code Section 1.08 states that:

"A promise or agreement made on consideration of marriage or nonmarital conjugal cohabitation is not enforceable unless the promise or agreement or a memorandum of the promise or agreement is in writing and signed by the person obligated by the promise or agreement."

The Texas Business Code allows parties to enter agreements in consideration of "nonmarital conjugal cohabitation." To be enforceable, these contracts or agreements must be:

- In writing and
- Signed by those who are affected by the agreement.

The Texas Legislature specifically stated that this provision was enacted to curb the number of palimony cases entering the family courts.

Oral agreements will likely not be upheld. At least one court has held that an oral agreement is not enforceable, *Zaremba v. Cilburn.*

Why a Cohabitation Agreement Maybe a Good Idea

As illustrated in the two examples I gave above, when you are living with someone else and are NOT planning to be married, sometimes lines blur and the couple starts making financial decisions as if they were married.

Then if the relationship does not work out, the couple is left with questions regarding who is responsible for any joint debts and who owns the assets. If not careful, someone might be significantly hurt financially.

The problem is partly because the characterization of property acquired by unmarried cohabitants is less clear than that of married couples. Married couple's ownership of property is governed by marital and community property laws.

Under community property laws, it does not matter whose name is on the property in most cases it is still owned by both parties in the marital relationship. This is not true for an unmarried couple.

One solution is a written cohabitation agreement that is signed and meets all the formalities of a regular contract. A cohabitation agreement allows an unmarried couple to legally spell out their rights and obligations toward each other.

Cohabitation agreements can be useful when:

- One of the parties dies
- If the cohabitants decide to end their relationship
- In governing the affairs of the couple while living together
- Generally, cohabitation can be used to:
- State the couple is not married and should not be considered married
- How expenses are to be paid
- Who is responsible for what during the living arrangement?
- Who pays the lease or the mortgage?
- Will the couple share any financial accounts such as a joint checking account?
- Identifies assets and debts, and who owns them
- What property is separate property or jointly owned?
- How the property will be distributed, should the couple split up
- Support Payments

What about Medical Decisions and Estate Planning?

Couples also sometimes have concerns regarding estate planning and medical care. Generally, someone who lives with another is not considered an heir under the law, and they do not have any rights to make medical decisions the way a legal spouse would.

If this is a concern, then you may want to consider in addition to a cohabitation agreement obtaining:

- Estate planning and
- Power of attorneys

Defenses to Cohabitation Agreements

The defenses to cohabitation agreements are those available under general contract law rather than the limited defenses available against premarital and postmarital agreements under the Family Code.

Common law defenses include:

- Fraud
- Repudiation
- Duress
- Mistake
- Unconscionability and
- Ratification.

If you are considering moving in together with your paramour or loved one, then you should think seriously about entering into a cohabitation agreement to protect yourself and eliminate uncertainty regarding your rights and duties to each other. A cohabitation can also provide a measure of security in the event the relationship terminates.

CHAPTER 30

CONCLUSION

L ife does not always work out the way you would like. You do not always get the results of what you do or what your spouse does. At the end of the day, it does not matter. The things that happen affect you. The courtroom and divorce often have been compared to a battleground. Some of the dirty tricks mentioned in this book seem absurd or foolish. But they are very real and they happen all the time.

During difficult times, it can be hard to take the high road. You may feel angry, upset, and emotion, and what is going on may tempt you to lash out and hurt your spouse. If you do, then your spouse may feel like they need to do same to you as well and a vicious cycle may begin.

This book was written to make it readers aware of possible dirty tricks in a divorce so that they can be defended against, and in many cases, they turned around against the spouse who tried to play the dirty trick.

It is important to realize that hurting your spouse ultimately hurts you as well. It hurts your children. Helping your spouse is often the last thing you feel like doing. However, it often helps you and your children. It helps even when it feels like it is not doing any good.

This is not to suggest that we encouraged doing nothing when a spouse who has had a dirty trick played on them. Doing nothing about a problem is often the worst approach. It allows a spouse to run over the other spouse.

To turn around the tricks mentioned in this book requires a proactive approach to stop the trick, or minimize the damage, and then show the court what is happening. What you do during a divorce matter sets the stage for how you will get through the rest of your life.

Once this is understood, it helps you understand how the manner you need to interact with your soon to be ex-spouse to protect your family and the quality of your relationships after the divorce is over. If you still have questions after reading this book and you need a personalized plan and answers regarding your situation, you can accomplish this by contacting an attorney at our law firm.

DO NOT MAKE THIS DECISION BY YOURSELF!

I hope this book has given you a better understanding of what to expect and how to protect your right to get fair treatment. I hope you have been introduced to enough concepts and legal principles to picture your future and how to begin navigating toward success. Thank you for investing your time with me.

I'd like to return the favor and offer you something in kind. Normally, I charge clients $375 an hour for my time. However, if you call my office and mention that you've read this book, I would be happy to waive that charge and provide an initial consultation for free.

You've experienced uncertainty, sadness, and frustration. Allow me to help restore your peace of mind. Knowledge is power. With my help, you can gain the knowledge to take back control and shape the future you deserve.

Please call my team now at (281) 720-3646 to schedule your consultation. I am looking forward to helping you put the past behind you and enjoy a brighter and more hopeful future.

Take action today toward
YOUR NEW FUTURE!

Call our office today:
Make your appointment for a
FREE CONSULTATION
(a $375 value)

Call:
(281) 720-3646
or visit:

www.bryanfagan.com

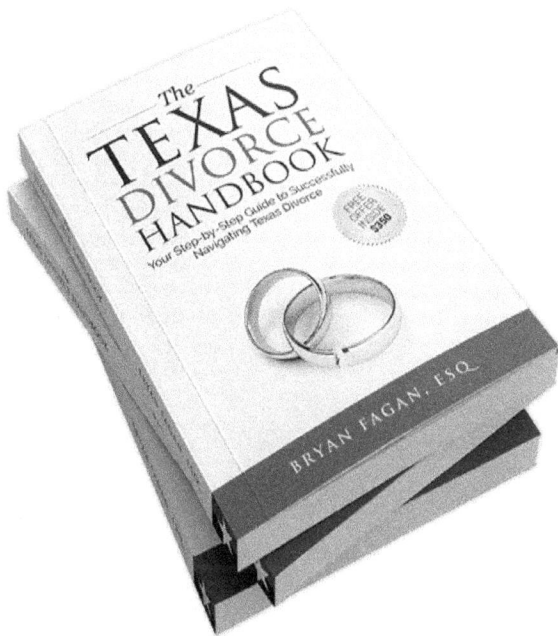

THE MOST INCREDIBLE FREE GIFT EVER

Learn How to Claim a Free Copy of My First Book
"The Texas Divorce Handbook"
FREE GIFT
Call our office today:

Call:
(281) 720-3646
or visit:
https://www.bryanfagan.com/New-Book.aspx

ABOUT THE AUTHOR

Attorney Bryan J. Fagan, of the Law Offices of Bryan Fagan, has spent most of his law career specializing in family law. He is a certified member of the College of the State Bar of Texas which is an honorary society established in 1982 by the Supreme Court of Texas. In his online posts and books, he succeeds in taking the complex language of the law and making it understandable to the general public. 25 Dirty Tricks to Guard Against and How to Counter Them is Bryan's second book. The Texas Divorce Handbook, Volume One was published in 2017.

www.ingramcontent.com/pod-product-compliance
Lightning Source LLC
Chambersburg PA
CBHW021923190326
41519CB00009B/888